PRAISE FOR *AMERICAN SEOUL*

"As she takes us across three continents, from childhood to middle age, Helena Rho shares the raw truth of what it's meant to strive for decades to be a good daughter, sister, mother, wife, and physician, all the while navigating the contradictory demands of Eastern and Western cultures. This is a powerfully heartfelt story about seeking the gravity of a place to belong while overcoming regrets and losses along the way. Her honesty is searing and, in the end, inspiring."

—Julia Glass, author of *Vigil Harbor* and the National Book Award–winning *Three Junes*

"In her devastating memoir, *American Seoul*, Helena Rho underscores the central truth of being alive: that while we are often helpless to prevent our suffering at the hands of others, we are not helpless to reimagine ourselves, to invent ourselves anew. There are second acts in American lives, and Rho beautifully teaches us what living means after the anguish. She is among the rarest of memoirists who can alchemize experience into art."

—William Giraldi, author of *The Hero's Body*

"A compelling coming-of-age story of women confronting clashing cultures and helpless alienation written with passion and heroic honesty."

—Lee Gutkind, editor and founder of *Creative Nonfiction* magazine

"In her riveting debut memoir, *American Seoul*, Helena Rho writes, 'Perhaps everyone has a flaming wreckage of a life. We can choose to watch it burn. Or we can take the jagged pieces and make a new life with the repaired seams evident, stark and startling and beautiful.' Here in my margin, I wrote, 'Ars memoria,' by which I meant, This is what a memoirist does—what the best memoirists do: they cauterize their words in those flames. Here in this passage, Rho foreshadows herself, for she has written her life as a book that is stark and startling and beautiful."

—Julie Marie Wade, author of *Wishbone: A Memoir in Fractures* and *Just an Ordinary Woman Breathing*

"*American Seoul* is a redemptive, often harrowing, and irresistible memoir. Helena Rho handles the complexities of deceit, betrayal, and dire family secrets with intelligence, grace, and courage. Just when you think things can't get worse, they get worse. But Helena clears the wreckage and moves on to become the person, the writer, she dreamed of being. This is a story so good, so exquisitely told, you'll want to stand up and cheer when you've finished."

—John Dufresne, author of *No Regrets, Coyote*

"A heart-filled, hard-won, and transcendent story of immigration and the generations after by a woman raised in a culture of high expectations. Exhausted, emotionally drained, and suffering from personal and intergenerational trauma, the author must also navigate rivers of the many personal, cultural, and professional ideals of what it means to be strong and confident, humble and self-sacrificing. Successful. Rho became a doctor—for others—and then a writer—for herself—and in making that choice created a way to remake her life. She wrote her way back to her Korean-ness, to wholeness, to becoming Heeseon again, and in doing so brings us all back to wholeness, compassion, and kindness."

—Jenny Forrester, author of *Narrow River, Wide Sky*

"Helena Rho's *American Seoul* is the triumphant story of one woman's fight to reclaim herself, her body, her Korean identity, and her right to tell her story. Rho shows us the cost of being a daughter in a family that prefers sons, a Korean immigrant in an America that celebrates whiteness, and a doctor when her heart longed for a life in the arts. Thankfully, Rho bravely challenged and ultimately discarded the toxic ideas that almost broke her body and her spirit. *American Seoul* is a gift to the world and a light for anyone still searching for a way out of a life that chafes the spirit."

—Christie Tate, *New York Times* bestselling author of *Group*

"Helena Rho's strength is unmistakable from the first pages of her ferocious memoir. Weaving threads of love, trauma, family, and the sometimes long, long journey toward home, Rho shows us how we can be made and unmade and made again. *American Seoul* is an unflinching chronicle of womanhood, motherhood, and selfhood, told with stark honesty and grace. This book is aria, howl, and lullaby—an unforgettable song."

—Chelsea Biondolillo, author of *The Skinned Bird*

"In her moving memoir, *American Seoul*, Helena Rho writes unflinchingly about misogyny, racism, and abuse. Her beautiful prose fuels a clear-eyed exploration of her life and its joys and challenges. A memorable debut."

—Cari Luna, author of *The Revolution of Every Day*

"*American Seoul* is a memoir that uncovers the in-between moments of a life—the shock of a car accident and the fluidity of a mind on the move in the milliseconds of the collision; the speculative spaces of the past in Korea to understand the frailties of parents; the abuse one endures and the trauma that shadows. Helena Rho shares her multiple lives: daughter, mother, wife, doctor, woman. It is a breathtaking tango that circles cultural identity, self-doubt and worth, and the vulnerabilities of living in a country that gives little and takes a lot."

—Ira Sukrungruang, author of *This Jade World*

"Helena Rho's *American Seoul* is as breathtaking as it is wise. This is the story of one brave woman's journey through family, culture, and identity. In the journey from discipline and intellect to compassion and creativity, Helena generously maps out for us how much can be taken as well as how much can be given when one must escape cultural and familial inscription in order to live fully, love fully, and thrive. Sometimes stepping off the path takes more than a leap of faith. Sometimes the leap takes your whole heart."

—Lidia Yuknavitch, author of *The Chronology of Water*

American Seoul

American Seoul

a memoir

HELENA RHO

Little
a

Published by Little A, New York

www.apub.com

Amazon, the Amazon logo, and Little A are trademarks of Amazon.com, Inc., or its
affiliates.

ISBN-13: 9781542035576 (hardcover)
ISBN-10: 1542035570 (hardcover)

ISBN-13: 9781542035552 (paperback)
ISBN-10: 1542035554 (paperback)

A portion of this book originally appeared, in a slightly different form, in
Fourth Genre: Explorations in Nonfiction.

A portion of this book originally appeared, in a slightly different form, in *Solstice:
A Magazine of Diverse Voices.*

A portion of this book originally appeared, in a slightly different form, in *Sycamore Review.*

A portion of this book originally appeared, in a slightly different form, in the
WOVEN series in *Entropy* magazine.

A portion of this book originally appeared, in a slightly different form, in *805 Lit + Art.*

A portion of this book originally appeared, in a slightly different form, in *Crab
Orchard Review.*

A portion of this book originally appeared, in a slightly different form, in *Post Road.*

Cover design by David Drummond

Printed in the United States of America

First edition

To my mother, Kang Hyun Soon

Table of Contents

AUTHOR'S NOTE

I have written this memoir using my memory, my notes, court documents, and the help of some of the people involved. I've changed most of the names to protect the identities of innocent people and to maintain their privacy. This memoir is my story, not anyone else's, told with as much honesty as I could muster. But memory is fallible.

Prologue

The early morning of Friday, August 29, 2003, in the Shadyside neighborhood of Pittsburgh was sunny but not warm, the waning of summer in the slight chill of the air. I was lying in bed, the scent of magnolias drifting through the window from the old tree outside, thinking of the coming Labor Day weekend, the shopping I had to do to make *bulgogi* beef barbecue. A favorite of my children. But first I was going to a yoga class. So when I slipped out of bed, I put on an athletic tank top and leggings, pulling on loose linen pants over the form-fitting leggings, which would be too revealing for my comfort when I dropped off my son at preschool at the JCC and my daughter at Chatham University for her last day of summer camp. As I passed my daughter's room on my way to my son's room at the end of the second-floor hallway of our Victorian house, I called to her to please get dressed. Liam was already awake, out of his trundle bed, playing with his toy cars. "Let's get ready," I said. He smiled up at me, his tiny front teeth flashing white.

Later, downstairs in the kitchen, my children ate Honey Nut Morning O's out of small metal IKEA bowls, drinkable strawberry yogurts within easy reach, a plate of fresh-cut strawberries to share at the center of the round wood table. They complained that they had the same breakfast every weekday morning, fun items like pancakes or waffles reserved for the weekend. But I said that wasn't true. Sometimes the yogurt was blueberry flavored, and sometimes the fruit was peach or pear or apple or raspberry. I had read somewhere that children, with their myelinating brains, needed "power" breakfasts—multigrain cereal, yogurt, and fruit. As a pediatrician, I prided myself on doing the right things for my children—whatever that meant.

Always running late, I left the breakfast dishes in the deep metal sink and hurried my kids to my silver sedan parked on the street outside our home, buckling my son into his car seat. Erin, at age seven, still needed a booster seat because she was so short but could manage the seat belt on her own. I drove into Squirrel Hill and up the winding road onto Chatham's campus, then waited in the car line until Erin, shouting, "Bye, Mom!" bolted out of the car at the entrance of the university's music and arts building. I smiled at Liam through my rearview mirror. "Now it's your turn, buddy." He smiled back. At age three, he wasn't as talkative as his sister. He clutched his favorite metal station wagon, painted forest green, in his hand.

Parking at the JCC was challenging that morning, requiring me to circle the garage several times. Liam's classmates were already all present and engaged in play when we stepped in the door of the large, bright room. I waved to the preschool teacher, gave Liam a kiss, and left. I was grateful I still had time before yoga started at nine o'clock.

Driving down Fifth Avenue in Shadyside, I was amused by the sight of one particular jogger on the sidewalk. My kids and I called her "the Flailer," an unkind reference to her peculiar style of running—her arms and legs flinging out, seemingly uncoordinated yet propelling her forward. "Good thing there's no one running next to her," my daughter would marvel, craning her neck while my son would laugh and clap. A few blocks farther, the traffic signal changed from green to yellow and I pressed on the brake. For a moment, my car slowed.

In order to describe what happened next in any coherent manner, I have to pretend that it happened in slow motion. I remember looking up at the red light and wondering why I was still moving, because my right foot was locked on the brake. At the same time, I felt shattering pain in my back, my chest slamming onto the steering wheel. I caught sight of a woman's horrified face in the rearview mirror. Trees spun past me out my driver's-side window, a blur of green. When all motion stopped, both my hands were gripping the steering wheel and I was staring at the car's clock. My first thought was, *Oh no, I'm going to be late for yoga.* I looked up at the windshield and expected it to be broken. I had heard the shattering of glass, the smashing of metal, the screeching of tires. I was holding my breath. I felt like my body was still being flung around like a rag doll, my head whipping back and forth. My vision blurred; I squeezed my eyes shut. A man ran to my driver's-side window and asked, "Are you okay?" Except his words sounded like they were echoing down a tunnel. I looked down at my hands still clenched around the steering wheel. "Yes, of course," I answered, convinced that if I couldn't see any cuts, any blood, then I must be fine. I ignored the throbbing ache spreading through my back, the stiffness in my neck.

I don't remember how I got out of my car. I do remember standing on the sidewalk, astonished that the red SUV that had hit me had a completely crushed front end, the hood folded in like an accordion. The bumper had fallen off, and the headlights were hollow. I caught the scent of hydrangeas and ended up staring at an entire row of those bushes, which served as a privacy fence for a house on Fifth Avenue. I tasted metal in my mouth and dabbed my tongue on the back of my hand, trying to find the source of bleeding, only to see clear saliva. I stood at one spot on the sidewalk, squinting against the sun, marveling at how beautiful the day was—no clouds, just clear, bright light. Everything else around me was chaos.

I remember at some point wondering why there were so many fire trucks at the intersection, the sirens of fire engines and police cars and ambulances competing against one other, a cacophony of sound. I remember glass shards glinting on the asphalt, the boots of the emergency workers crunching through them. My head hurt and I just wanted to go home. When an EMT told me to get in the ambulance,

I demurred. I remember his concerned blue eyes and the frown on his face as he said, "You're in shock. You need to go to the ER." I told him I was a pediatrician and would know if something was wrong with my body. I insisted I was fine. He kept shaking his head.

The drive back home took more than five minutes, but I have no memory of it. I remember feeling deep relief when I saw my dark-blue Victorian house. I don't remember where I parked on the street. I remember telling myself, *I'm fine, I'm fine,* even as I clutched at my back because the pain was excruciating. My neck and shoulder muscle had seized, and I couldn't turn my head.

I made it to the kitchen before I fell to the floor, my tears overflowing, obscuring everything in front of me, blurring the sight of mucus pouring out of my nose onto my hands, the liquid warm and sticky. I could hear the jagged cries coming from my throat, low at first and then rising in crescendo until I couldn't recognize the high-pitched wails as my own. As much as I wanted to, I couldn't seem to stop. I was a small, inconsolable heap on the wood floor of my kitchen, unable to move, light streaming through the tall windows of the Victorian.

Through the years, I have been asked many times—too many to count, or maybe I'm too lazy to count—why I left the practice of medicine. "I wasn't happy" seemed like a frivolous answer when I first left medicine in 2004, so instead I said, "I've always wanted to write." I didn't say that I wanted to be *a writer.* That would have been too presumptuous, my strict Korean upbringing ingrained and insisting that I be modest. Those who are not humble will be punished, my mother had told me, time and time again. It seemed that to my mother, the biggest sin you could commit was being utterly confident about your self-worth. That and marrying a white man. She turned out to be right about the white man.

Whenever I was asked, "Why leave medicine now?" I would usually shrug my shoulders. Sometimes I would joke it was a midlife crisis, because I was forty years old when I left the practice of pediatrics. All those years, I didn't know that I was avoiding talking about the traumatic car accident that tore my neck and shoulder muscle and herniated two discs in my lower back, leading to chronic back pain, tingling and numbness down my right leg, a limp, and a stiffness in my neck that persists today.

My body bears the scars of trauma—the sexual abuse when I was eight and nine years old, the cultlike conditions of being raised by an immigrant Korean mother with major depression, then the nightmare of marrying an emotionally and physically abusive man. The trauma of being sexually harassed on an almost-daily basis as a medical student. The trauma of being racially discriminated against by my fellow doctors and the institutions that hired me as a pediatric resident and then an attending pediatrician. The trauma of being oppressed by the white patriarchal court system, which wrongly insists it is a justice system while punishing women and people of color. Sometimes I want to burst into song—Pink's "I Am Here"—just to assert my presence. My survival.

Nine years after my car accident, in 2012, during a divorce deposition in a conference room with my ex-husband's attorney, tears sprang up unexpectedly and my voice cracked as I described my car accident. The lawyer's intention had been to lead me to admit how caring and generous my ex-husband had been in allowing me to temporarily leave the practice of pediatrics, and how irresponsible I was not to return when I was supposedly able-bodied. How negligent I was not to be contributing to our family income. Apparently, raising two children and writing a book wasn't enough. Apparently, the combination of my ex-husband's salary as the chief of pulmonary at a New York City–area hospital and his prolific lecturing fees paid by pharmaceutical companies wasn't enough. Hundreds of thousands of dollars. I testified that

I still had back pain. I still had pain radiating down my leg; I still had numbness in my foot. I just didn't complain about it all the time. I think it was the first time I articulated the direct connection between my car accident and my leaving medicine. Cause and effect. And I said it without shame, without lingering guilt that I had abandoned a perfectly good career. But I was surprised that I had reacted to the past trauma with such emotion. I didn't realize then that our bodies carry our trauma.

Now when people ask me why I left medicine, I say, "Well, it started with a car accident. But it was really ten thousand things." Ten thousand is an important number for Koreans. For instance, we say that Korea is *a land of ten thousand mountains* because Korea does have many mountains, although probably not ten thousand. And during the Joseon dynasty, emperors received ten thousand blessings for a long life. The word for "ten thousand" in Korean is *mahn*. And *mahn* is part of another word, *mahnsae*, which means "live long" and also "victory." Leaving medicine and embracing freedom and joy felt like a journey of ten thousand leaps and shuffles. But it was a victory.

I realize now I couldn't have left medicine of my own volition. I needed to be literally crashed out of it. I carried too much guilt and shame to make the conscious decision to leave behind the dark unhappiness of my life—a career I didn't want, a husband who was abusive, a yearning to write what I couldn't say out loud. I needed a catastrophic event to set into motion my journey of self-discovery; otherwise I never would have set my foot on that path. I never would have returned home to Seoul.

Chapter 1
Crossroad

Korea, August 1961. She stood at the crossroad. Not weeping, just leaking a constant stream of tears. Dust from a passing car covered her face, her clothes, despite her turning away, closing her eyes. She glanced down, brushed at the red-brown film blanketing her yellow dress. It was useless. The relentless sun, the blazing blue sky, summer in the southern inland of Korea was unforgiving. The army barracks, still visible in the distance, seemed to undulate in the heat. Nothing marked the bus stop at the crossroad. No shelter, not even a bench. She stood under the withering sun and waited. Two small suitcases at her feet contained her worldly possessions. Tears created rivulets down her dirt-coated cheeks. Eight months pregnant, she was returning to the home of her parents in disgrace.

A failure. The humiliation of crawling back to her father's house pregnant, after a ruined marriage, was too much to bear. She squeezed her eyes shut. She never thought she would be in this position. At least her friends would be surprised. "Hyun Soon, the perfect princess" was their nickname for her. Not only did it speak to her privileged world of servants and gardeners and trips to the cinema to see the latest American film, but it also described her single-minded desire to be the heroine of the larger-than-life movies she loved.

But it all came to a stop with her marriage. *The start of her husband's obligation to the army, as mandated by Korean law, marked the beginning of their life together. She, who had never seasoned soup because of the servants in her father's employ, learned to cook in one-room barracks. She'd never thought the sewing and knitting required of her, a good Korean daughter, would be used for practical things like maternity dresses and blankets, rather than decorative things like doilies and teapot covers. She hung her wash outside on a clothesline, like a peasant of the lowest class.*

Her husband was a doctor and a yang ban, *the coveted aristocratic class of Korean society. His family lineage could be traced back to the daughter of an emperor of the Joseon dynasty. Her ancestors were from the merchant class. Their marriage marked an elevation in status for her family. As befitting more modern times, their marriage was not arranged. Her cousin and his best friend engineered their "meeting," which occurred only after the approval of both sets of parents. During their courtship, they were not permitted to be alone. She remembered her trepidation during their meetings, stealing looks at him with her head bent and eyes lowered. Keungnae was handsome, a little too dark skinned to be considered gorgeous, but still good-looking. He seemed to have a lively personality: outgoing and warm, if a little impulsive. He was a surgeon and dedicated to his work. She so admired passion and purpose—qualities that were, after all, forbidden to her. As a woman, she was not supposed to harbor ambition. She was supposed to marry, have children.*

She knew he was the jangsohn, *the oldest son of the oldest son, that all-important, highest-ranking male of his generation. A patriarchal line that stretched back five hundred years. His family expected her to have a boy to continue the succession. But she was not worried. Her mother had borne three sons. She was certain she would give birth to the next jangsohn. And when she had a son, she would become a beloved daughter-in-law.*

Chaperoned by her family, they ate together, took tea together, and once went to the theater to watch An Affair to Remember *with Cary Grant and Deborah Kerr. She loved the cinema, and he seemed to share her enthusiasm.*

He even said that their romance was just like the movie, but he smiled and added that it would not be a tragedy. That was the moment she fell in love.

Their courtship lasted several months. He was completing his medical training in Seoul, many miles from her family home, and visited her on weekends. He seemed tired most times they were together, but he always asked about her interests: gardening, embroidery, books. She was too shy to tell him she wanted to write a novel. She remembered one particular encounter early in their courtship, when she was seated across from him at a low black lacquered table, offering him tea. His hands brushed against hers as he took the delicate celadon cup from her. Her skin tingled from his touch. He thanked her with a charming smile and said, "I hear you are a great reader of classics—Shakespeare and Hemingway. I admire intelligence in women. My mother loves to read, but alas, I am ignorant about literature. You must teach me to be smarter." She had blushed. He was a doctor; she was only a teacher who'd studied English literature in college.

Perhaps it was not everything she had expected, and he was not really a fan of the cinema, but they had made a good life together in ten months of marriage. Until last night. She shook her head at the memory of the moment, feeling like Susan Hayward, who closes her eyes when faced with blatant evidence of her lover's duplicity in Back Street.

She had been emptying his pockets, as usual, before washing his pants. She was smiling because he always kept the oddest things—not just cigarettes and change but torn pieces of paper, toothpicks, an earpiece to his stethoscope. She found something new: a handkerchief dirtied with red lipstick. She never wore red lipstick. Pink was more modest, more respectable for a married woman. Her chest tightened and compressed. She consciously drew in each breath, concentrating on pulling in air and then pushing it out. She felt ice cold in the suffocating heat. She dragged herself to their bed and lay down with the covers shrouding her head. She watched the light fade from the walls. She found the dark comforting.

She heard the jangle of keys, the opening of the front door, the surprise of her husband as he stepped into an unlit house. Yet she did not move. He

3

came into their tiny bedroom, which barely fit a double bed and dresser, solicitous about her health: Did she feel all right? She answered that she had a migraine. He was aware of her infirmity. He asked if he could do anything for her. She curled her body away from him and said no. She almost expected him to sense that something was terribly wrong. In An Affair to Remember, Cary Grant realizes something is amiss when Deborah Kerr fails to stand up as he is leaving, a blanket covering her useless legs. Then he knows.

Her husband ate, showered, and went to sleep next to her with only a brief squeeze of her arm. He snored peacefully. She wept next to him. In the morning, with her eyes puffy, she told him she was sick. He put on his uniform and left for the army hospital as usual, not sensing anything awry. As she lay in bed staring at the wall, imagining it imprinted with red lipstick marks, the heat of rage flared in her chest and consumed her. It did not matter that she was pregnant and cumbersome. She refused to be humiliated this way.

Although she worshipped her beloved father, she had witnessed her mother's anguish in the face of his infidelity. And she had sworn never to let it happen to her. Standing at the door with her suitcases in hand, she looked back at the sparsely furnished and starkly decorated house. Cement floors, gray concrete walls, rectangular windows covered with simple white curtains, all part of standard army-issue housing. But this had been her home for the past year. Some of her defiance left her and her shoulders sagged. Still, she picked up her bags and walked to the crossroad.

She waited. Sometimes, soldiers passing by in jeeps would ask if they could take her somewhere. She just shook her head. No one could take her back to her life. To before. The exact moment she pulled that handkerchief from his pocket repeated over and over in slow motion. Like the scene from Back Street *when Susan Hayward misses a crucial flight, calls her lover at home, and discovers that John Gavin is married and, ironically, has been unfaithful to her.*

She was jolted back to her life by the insistent sound of a blaring horn and a shouting voice. Certain that someone of low class, surely a peasant, was exhibiting this unseemly behavior, she was taken aback at the sight of her husband frantically waving his arm. He came to a screeching halt, jumped out, and ran to her. He pulled her into his arms. She let herself feel the warmth of security, the renewal of hope. Then she remembered. A chill swept into her body. Her head reared back. She pulled out of his embrace. She resisted the temptation to pretend that this was the final scene in An Affair to Remember, with Cary Grant and Deborah Kerr back in each other's arms.

"I came home to check on you and you were gone! The woman next door said she saw you leave with luggage. What happened?" His words tumbled out in a torrent.

"I decided to leave," she said, turning away from him.

"What kind of answer is that?" He grabbed her arm. "I am your husband! I demand an explanation!"

She felt frozen in ice, unable to summon any of the emotions of yesterday. An absence of feeling. She wondered if this was what death felt like.

"Yeubo," he pleaded.

Yeubo was what he called her, and what she called him in return. It implied intimacy. A word reserved for only one other person in the world. She used to take pride in that word, evidence that they belonged together.

"Is it something I did? Is it something I said?" he persisted.

She stared at stones with dust veneers by the side of the road, willing him to stop. Their marriage was over.

"Please tell me what's wrong. I love you," he said, anguish in his voice, his brows furrowed, his hands haphazardly running through his thick dark hair.

She flinched. A dam burst inside her. "I can't stand the lies! You don't love me, you never did!" Scorched by the flame of anger, she sobbed. She did not resist when he took her in his arms again. With her face buried in his chest, she whispered, "I found it. I found the lipstick on your handkerchief."

5

"What are you talking about?" He pulled out a folded linen square, clean and white.

She pushed him away. "I mean the one I found in your pocket yesterday."

He didn't hesitate. He flashed a smile, his teeth white and even. "That wasn't mine. A friend was afraid to take it home so I told him I would wash it for him. I forgot to tell you."

She looked at him, wary. But his face was open and guileless; his lips smooth and curved. His long fingers caressed her face, his touch warm and light against her cheeks.

"You are imagining things." He wrapped his arm around her shoulders and guided her to the jeep.

She wanted to believe him. In her favorite movies, heartbreak was always averted at the last possible moment. Susan Hayward chooses moral ambiguity and remains with John Gavin, even though he's married, because she loves him. Cary Grant stays with Deborah Kerr, even after her car accident, because he loves her. Her husband loved her. Why else would he chase after her, like Cary Grant pursued Deborah Kerr?

But the whisper of doubt would not go away.

This is the way I picture the story my mother told me for the first time when I was ten years old and repeated many times. The image still sears my heart: the heat, the dust, the deserted bus stop. My pregnant mother crying, my desperate father begging. Perhaps the end of their marriage was inevitable, regardless of the fact that they would have three more children, including me, after their first child was born.

My mother told me the story again while she and my father were divorcing, more than thirty years after that day at the crossroad. She described the scene: She is glancing back at the crossroad, as my father is tugging her away, when the bus finally arrives. A single passenger gets out. The driver waits, for what seems to my mother an eternity, then shuts the door. As she watches, the bus lurches away in a cloud of dust. Her chance evaporates in the heat of inland summer. When she told me her story for the first time, the look in her eyes was one of infinite regret.

And even at ten, I could not stop myself from asking, "Why did you stay?"

I think she told me the story as an example of how she became trapped in her unhappy marriage. To explain that she had no choices. Instead, I heard her story as a cautionary tale: Korean men are not to be trusted. Not that there were a lot of Korean boys or men around me in the parts of America where I spent my young adulthood. But I had heard my mother complain countless times about my father drinking too much, smoking too much, and being unfaithful. And the Korean dramas I watched with her portrayed most Korean men as feckless, abandoning their pregnant lovers only to return years later and not very apologetic. I thought that if I didn't marry a Korean man, I would be safe.

About a month after I started medical school, my mother asked me if there were any Korean boys in my class. I told her there were only a few, and she said, *"You must date one of them. You're twenty-three years old. You must find a husband soon."*

"What are you talking about? You never wanted me to date the entire time I was in college—you said boys were only a distraction from my studies."

"That was college."

"That was only a year ago. Now you want me to get married as soon as possible?"

"Not right away. As soon as you finish medical school."

"Great. You're willing to give me four years to get married. But I need to find the right man soon?"

"A Korean man."

"Why? You hate Dad. Why would you want me to marry a Korean man?"

"Of course you must marry Korean. It is who you are."

My mother thought nothing of how contradictory she was being. My father had cheated on her several times during their marriage and caused her misery. My paternal grandfather had disliked her intensely and treated her like a servant, humiliating her. These were the stories I grew up hearing, and yet she wanted me to marry a Korean man. She had told me many times that my sisters and I did not act like good Korean daughters. That we were American, not Korean. It seemed to me that being Korean meant that you were doomed to a life of suffering, especially if you were a woman. One of the reasons I married my ex-husband was precisely because he was not Korean. Perhaps I was trying to change my fate. Instead, my fate was worse.

Chapter 2
The Last *Jangsohn*

Seoul, 1972. He sat on the chair, his shoulders hunched, his hands gripping the cold metal armrests. Through the large plate glass window, he watched his children running, weaving through the colorful garden, shrieking with delight. Four daughters. He turned his head and looked out the other side of the airport at the winged metal cylinder that would take them to Uganda, a country on the other side of the earth from where they were born. His head sank. His heart felt hollow.

While his relatives bade him farewell, his brother's navy-suited body stood like a shield against his father's black suit. But he knew the time was coming. He did not run when he saw his father's stout body striding toward him. He sat still as his father waited for him to look up. He stared at his father's black-polished shoes.

"Keungnae, what are you doing?" his father demanded.

He pretended ignorance. "I am trying to rest before a long journey."

"You are the jangsohn. You have responsibilities," his father said, his tone imperious.

All attempts at pretense dropped. He slumped in his chair, his slender fingers falling from the chrome supports. "Father, please, do not make this difficult."

"What you are doing is not right!"

He closed his eyes against the fury on his father's face. "Abeoji, I beg you, please, do not make this any harder than it has to be."

"Abandoning your family? Abandoning your home?" His father remained unyielding.

"I will not abandon my wife and daughters. Going to Uganda will be best for all of us." He crossed his arms, crumpling his new gray suit. He was weary of having the same conversation over and over again.

"Are you trying to punish me? I never suggested you leave your wife and children. I merely wanted you to have a son. We need the next jangsohn. Our family honor is at stake." His father's eyes, black and unblinking, drilled into his own pupils.

"By impregnating a woman from our village? A custom not practiced since the eighteenth century? A woman so poor she has no choice? If she has a son, we will take him away from her. If she has a daughter, she has another mouth to feed."

"We will pay her. And if she has a girl, we will give her more money. We will make things right."

His jaw clenched as he listened to his father's justifications, his unrelenting blindness to reason. His father was determined to get his way; he had always gotten his way before.

He knew his father had witnessed the dissolution of their ancestral home, the loss of face, the sudden need to work because his grandfather was an alcoholic who had gambled away the family fortune. Abeoji had found himself destitute, but his years of study as a privileged son of the aristocracy made him a natural fit for teaching. Abeoji had told the story many times of how he started as a lowly teacher but quickly advanced to principal and then superintendent. He treated life as though it were a game to be won.

He tried to appeal to his father's vanity. "Uganda is a great opportunity for me. The kind of money they are paying, and the good I can do as a professor of medicine at the university. I can be famous, like Albert Schweitzer, with a good reputation. My classmates from Yonsei will be envious."

"You had a good position here in Seoul. It is because of her, isn't it? You should never have married that woman. She was beneath you, of a lower class. And she couldn't even bear a son. Who has use for such a woman? I never liked her. Your mother did, poor misguided soul."

His mother had passed of stomach cancer a year earlier. Sometimes he wondered if her gentle constitution could not bear his father's oppressiveness. "Please, do not speak of Uhmonni in that way. She was a wonderful woman, a good wife and mother."

"I am not disrespecting your mother. I miss her care. She was just a bad judge of character."

"Father, please, do not malign my wife."

An image of his wife flashed through his mind: her petite, curvaceous body in a black-and-white dress. That's what she wore the first time he met her, on their double date with his best friend and her female cousin. She was shy, but her smile was luminescent.

"Why did your fifth child have to be a girl? If only that boy had lived. But he was too little." His father's stridence diminished, his voice fading in volume.

"My younger brother will care for you now." He tried to maintain a steady gaze, but the delicate muscle under his right eye twitched, rippling his vision.

"Keungnae-ya, don't do this." His father's round, usually implacable face creased, his lips about to quiver.

The sight of his father so anguished was new to him. And the sound of his name used so pleadingly, the suffix a sign of affection, almost unspooled him. He swallowed with effort.

"I failed to have a son. I am sorry."

He stood up, a half head taller than his father. He leaned down, stretching his long, thin arms. "Please, let us say farewell. When I return, we can start anew."

His father's black-suited body stood erect, immovable as a statue.

He drew in a long breath, summoning every cell in his body for strength. He turned from his father and walked away, his footsteps echoing on the cold tile floor.

∽

There is a picture of my father when he was twenty-seven years old, cradling my oldest sister, an infant, against his shoulder. His chest is broad, his head erect. He stands tall among dune grass, staring out at the water. His face is sleek, but there is a hint of an arc to his lips, as though a smile had burst forth immediately after the picture was taken. He is dressed in a T-shirt and fitted pants—I can't tell what color, because the photograph is black and white. The sun casts shadows behind him, but my father's face is brightly lit. He is striking. His dark, thick hair swept off his forehead, his nose straight, his jaw chiseled. Like a Korean Cary Grant. No wonder my mother fell in love with him.

The photograph must have been taken by my mother. I imagine they returned to Jeju Island, the site of their honeymoon, with their baby daughter. Maybe they were celebrating their one-year wedding anniversary. Perhaps my mother called out to him, *"Here! Look here at the camera!"* Maybe they laughed about the passage of time or how they'd forgotten that the East Sea was frigid in October. Their life held such promise: a handsome doctor and a beautiful young woman.

My father was born in 1934, while Korea was still under the merciless Japanese occupation, under which it would remain until 1945, the end of World War II. As a child, during the obliteration of Korean culture and language by colonizers, he learned to speak Japanese fluently, before his mother tongue. My father was a teenager during the Korean War. He told me that, as a seventeen-year-old, he drove an ambulance and worked as a medic, while the Americans and the Soviets and the Chinese fought over the Korean peninsula before the land of five thousand years fractured, along the 38th parallel, into North and

South Korea. And the two countries would go on disparate trajectories, no longer recognizable as a whole.

My father became a surgeon in Korea, his slender fingers perfectly suited to the nimble tasks of slicing, excising, sewing. He also had the focus that hours and hours of standing on his feet and cutting and repairing required.

In 1972, he answered the call for doctors to teach medical students and residents at Makerere University in Kampala, the capital city of Uganda. After Idi Amin, the notorious dictator, staged a military coup and seized control of Uganda in 1971, he expelled the "foreigners," as he called them—many second- and third-generation Indians, Pakistanis, and Bangladeshis living in Uganda, as well as the British expatriates who had stayed after the end of colonial rule—and found himself without an infrastructure to run his country. Amin traveled the world asking for help, and his generous financial incentives enticed people from all over the globe. The doctors came from Korea.

I pieced together the story of my father leaving for Uganda from my own memory, from fights I overheard between my parents, and from my aunt, who, when I saw her in 2006, told me that we left Korea because my parents couldn't have a son.

When Amin finally issued exit visas, all the Koreans immigrated to the United States. My father was poorly prepared to practice internal medicine in America, which demanded a different set of skills: a softer demeanor, fluidity in English. I have the same long fingers, but I chose pediatrics.

When I was twenty-seven years old, my father went to a federal penitentiary for Medicaid fraud. His imprisonment led to my parents' divorce. I rarely visited him. I was ashamed of him. Now, as a former practicing physician and someone who has been through the court system myself, I can see what happened. Yes, he prescribed methadone without too many questions. Maybe he did only a cursory physical exam. Maybe he slipped into complacency and didn't bother with too many details before writing for a controlled substance. But I think he was also trying to be compassionate to his patients, addicts withdrawing and in pain. He was a person of color caught in an unfair judicial system, his punishment harsher than a white doctor's might have been—eighteen months instead of a suspended sentence. My father found God in prison, became a born-again Christian. After his release, he led medical missions to a remote part of China near the North Korean border. The ethnic Koreans trapped in that region of China needed doctors. By then I was in my third year of pediatric residency.

A month after my wedding and about six months after my father's prison term, my mother called me on the phone.

"How much money did you receive?" she demanded in Korean.

"What money?"

"Your grandmother sent you six thousand dollars as a dowry." Her tone suggested I was acting like an idiot.

"I never got it."

"Are you sure? Halmoni said she gave it to your father when he was visiting from Seoul." Her voice rose an octave.

"I don't have it." My shoulders seized with dread.

"You understand that you will be expected to give the same amount to one of your younger cousins when he or she gets married."

My ignorance of Korean customs ambushed me. The knowledge that I had to gift six thousand dollars to some unknown cousin in a few years pressed into my chest, squeezing all the air out. I couldn't speak.

"Call your father."

I called my father.

"Dad, where is the money from Halmoni?"

"What money?"

"My wedding gift."

"Halmoni gave that money to me. She wanted to help me after all my hardship."

"Why would Mom's mother give you money?"

"The money was for me."

"That's not true."

"I needed it."

"You have to return that money to me."

"It's gone."

"What?"

"I spent it."

"How could you do this to me?"

Silence on his end.

"Goodbye, Dad." My hand covered my face, tears burning as they slipped down my throat.

At the time, I didn't know that conversation would be the last time I would talk to my father. He remarried another Korean woman, a widow with several children. He didn't invite me to his wedding, maybe because he knew I wouldn't go. He spent his last years split between Korea and America and occasionally contacted my sister Susan, who we all agreed was his favorite. It came as a shock when he was hospitalized with neurological issues about a year before his death and he claimed that I was his favorite daughter. Susan was devastated; my other two sisters were probably bitter but said nothing. I didn't believe him. When he passed away from heart ailments, I didn't attend his funeral. I was at a hospital waiting for a friend to come out of surgery from a mastectomy because of breast cancer. My sisters disapproved, even though I said that, as a physician, our father would understand: our obligation to the living supersedes our duty to the dead.

Because my father helped raise me, I learned that fathers did not necessarily love their children. I learned to accept very little attention from him. I learned that fathers didn't spend time with their children, didn't look out for their children. And I learned to expect that a husband would be selfish and careless and leave his children behind, with little expectation that he would support them either emotionally or financially.

The picture of my father standing tall in the dunes is lost. Along with so many prints in rectangles and squares, both black and white and Kodak color, fragments of our lives when we lived in Korea. I wonder what my father was thinking the moment that photograph on Jeju Island was taken as he looked out at the seemingly unending expanse of water. Did he feel content that his life was settled with a wife and child? Or was he less sanguine because his firstborn was not a boy? Did my father have any prickling that he would become the last jangsohn, the last oldest son, in an arc of ancestry curving back five hundred years to the daughter of an emperor?

Chapter 3
Blood Flamingos in Uganda

The first words I learned in English were *axe* and *basket*. As in, "A is for axe and B is for basket," said my English tutor. How we learned our ABCs was a peculiar quirk of being in Uganda, a former colony of the United Kingdom. My sisters and I were sitting around our tutor's dining room table, writing the words down on notebooks we were given for the occasion of our first English lesson. It was the summer of 1972. When my parents picked us up after our lesson, they asked how it had gone. *"Is English easy?"* they asked in Korean. My sisters and I laughed. *"It sounds strange,"* we answered. After that incident, I have no memory of not being able to speak English. It slid into my consciousness without me noticing. I read in English, I thought in English, and I spoke in English to everyone, even my Korean parents. But there must have been a period of transition, before I lost my Korean and was left only with English. Was this transformation slow and insidious? Or was it abrupt? Did I wake up one day in our stone-and-concrete house in Kampala and speak only English?

I had started first grade in Seoul in March 1972, but in September, because I had turned seven at the start of the Ugandan school year, which was modeled after the British school calendar, I began second grade without finishing first grade. I sat at the back of the classroom, not wanting to be noticed. But that wasn't possible because there were no other Korean students in my class and because of Bruno. I remember the other girls being jealous that the blond boy from Yugoslavia liked me and tried to stand next to me whenever we had to walk hand in hand from the classroom to the cafeteria or the playground. But I liked Daniel, the Ugandan boy with the gentle face and soft voice. I always held his hand tighter and wished it was for longer. He seemed to like me, but he never fought Bruno for a spot next to me like the other boys did. And I was told by the other girls how lucky I was that Bruno, with his blue eyes, had a crush on me. Lucky.

I'm lucky was what I thought when the twelve-year-old Korean boy shoved his hand into my underwear, his fingers rooting around. I flinched at first but then held my breath, kept still. We were lying next to one another in the middle of my parents' bed, my sisters on both sides. He had chosen me. My sister Susan, a classmate of his, had a crush on him, but he showed no interest in her. My eight-year-old self thought I should like him because he liked me.

The twelve-year-old and his younger sister were sleeping over because our parents were going to another party at the Korean embassy. In 1974, the Korean doctors and their wives in Kampala threw parties practically weekly, usually at the ambassador's house. My mother almost always complained that my father drank too much. She would only have a glass of wine in those days. One night they came home raging at one another. I hid under the bed with my sisters, holding my hands over my ears, but nothing could stop the sound of their shouting. She accused him of infidelity. He yelled that she was a frigid wife. My mother never drank alcohol after leaving Uganda. Their raging did not stop.

I think I was still holding my breath as the older boy fumbled with my labia, when we heard our mothers burst into the living room. We scrambled out of bed.

Squinting against the lights, I stood in the hallway, arrested by the sight of my mother crying. My mother shouted, or expressed her anger by thinning her lips, ferociously frowning, crossing her arms in front of her body. Sometimes she smiled. Rarely she laughed. But I had never seen her cry.

"He almost died," she said.

"Your husband is at the hospital and recovering. It is not that bad," the other Korean mother said.

What happened to my father? What is going on? I thought. But I didn't ask any questions. A good daughter was quiet and obedient.

"Children, your father was in a car accident. A truck in the opposite lane of the highway swerved in the rain and hit your parents' car. Your father was thrown through the windshield and hit his head. But he is fine," the other mother said.

"He is still unconscious! His head was soaked with blood. He is going to die," my mother wept.

I couldn't breathe. *What will happen to us?* I thought.

"Stop being melodramatic. Pull yourself together. You are going to frighten the children," the other mother admonished.

My mother kept weeping, but she stopped talking. The other woman comforted my sisters, who had started crying, but I didn't cry. My mother had told me time and time again that to cry was to be weak. I wasn't weak. A few days later, we visited my father in the hospital. He was smiling but his head was swathed in white bandages. When he came home a week later, I could see the stitches on his scalp and the angry pink flesh around it. I was grateful he had not died. We didn't talk about his accident again.

I used to tell people that my childhood in Uganda was idyllic. Sun-dappled days and mango trees in front yards and going on safari every August, while my father was on vacation for the month. I never spoke about the fear and dread behind all that sunshine. In 1975, my parents sold everything from china cabinets to clothes and we moved from our cinder block house on the outskirts of the capital into the Kampala International Hotel. It was supposed to be for only a few days, but the sojourn lasted for months while we waited for Idi Amin, the despotic ruler, to issue exit visas, so we could immigrate to the United States.

When we first moved into the International, my parents made it sound like a grand adventure: decadent living in a posh hotel. We didn't all have to share one bathroom anymore because my sisters and I had our own room. It had wall-length floor-to-ceiling windows opening onto a balcony with a lush garden below. My mother said we didn't have to clean our room. There was housekeeping, not to mention several dining rooms and an outdoor pool. I didn't know it then, but Amin, "the Butcher of Uganda," was guilty of countless human rights violations, including torture, executions, and mass killings. My parents pretended they weren't afraid, but I caught snatches of whispers between them: *Are we going to be allowed to leave at the end of this week? Next month? What if it becomes too dangerous?* I think now about how terrified my parents must have been, yet they said nothing to my sisters and me. Perhaps their fear obscured their judgment: they let a thirty-something-year-old man teach math to their thirteen-, eleven-, and nine-year-old daughters alone, unsupervised. Every week I came to dread our lessons. But I didn't say anything to my parents.

I was served elaborate meals in the dining room by Ugandan waiters in tuxedos and waistcoats, their hands encased in pristine white gloves. Silver twelve-piece place settings and crystal goblets were expected at dinner, along with girls and women in dresses, men and boys in jackets. My best dress, which I wore almost every night, was saffron yellow with white polka dots. My outfit was completed by white lace-topped socks and black dress shoes with a slight heel. I always tucked my long hair behind my ears before I went down to dinner. My mother sometimes let my sisters and me eat lunch in the garden surrounding the hotel swimming pool; perfectly composed sandwiches on white china, served on round glass tables, the children dripping wet on Bertoia Diamond chairs, icons of mid-century modern design. And we watched the latest English movies, like James Bond in *The Man with the Golden Gun*, in the hotel's lavish theater, complete with balcony seats in plush red velvet. On the surface, my life was charmed when I was nine years old, but underneath terror reigned. I became physically sick, my stomach seizing, every week just before the math tutor entered our suite, shouting a cheery greeting to my mother before she left for her room next door.

He pressed his stout fingers into the thin flesh of my arms, pulling me into his embrace in the dark cool of the hotel room. "Come to me, my beautiful!"

I fought his smelly cigarette breath, wriggling in his lap, frantically gasping for air.

Only moments before, I had been sitting on the balcony in sunshine, my head bent over a math workbook. My sister Susan had been inside the hotel room with our math tutor, going over her math homework. But it was now my turn. I walked as slowly as I could from the balcony, with its view over the hotel's colorful garden, into the room. As soon as the sliding door slid shut, he grabbed me.

I tried to push out of his lap, but he trapped me between his thighs. I held my breath.

"You are a sweet morsel!" he said, his lips making smacking noises against my neck, my cheeks.

I turned my head as far away from him as I could. But one of his kisses landed on my lips. I wanted to vomit, but I didn't cry.

"Stop fighting! Be a good girl," he cajoled, his arms around me like a steel cage I couldn't break out of.

I sat still, my head bowed, thinking that would bore him, that would make him stop.

Instead, he gripped both my hands in one of his and shoved the other into my underwear, peeling open my hairless labia. He moaned, thrusting his erect penis against my buttocks. I think I blanked out, because the next thing I remember is sitting on the balcony again, staring at scarlet blossoms in the hotel garden.

On the night of my father's car accident, I knew the older Korean boy shouldn't have grabbed me. I knew I had done something wrong.

But I could not say anything to my mother. My mother had said many times that if my sisters and I were good girls, then everything would be fine. We just had to listen to her and obey. Be good Korean daughters. When the math tutor assaulted me, I blamed myself. I was not a good girl. I had let a boy and then a man touch me.

Once, on safari, I'm not sure whether it was in Queen Elizabeth National Park or Murchison Falls National Park, I saw a terrible sight. On a lazy sunny afternoon, on a boat in a huge lake, I watched sunlight bounce off the shimmery surface, reflecting everywhere. The water seemed impenetrable. I was slumped against the boat railing, my head on my arms, the still water mesmerizing, the warmth lulling me almost to sleep. Suddenly I saw a crocodile's jaws rear out of the water, yawn open, and snap shut. A collective gasp erupted around me. I recoiled from the railing but couldn't stop watching. A flock of pink flamingos near the shoreline shrieked and flapped in the air. Below them, turbulent water churned as the crocodile disappeared underneath, successful in its attack. Even when the water calmed, the splatters of blood seemed to dye it red, clouds appearing overhead and obliterating the sun.

I swallowed the shame the same way the water seemed to swallow the crocodile, as if the violence had never happened. I shut it up inside a part of me that would not acknowledge what had happened until I was fifty years old. I thought that by not acknowledging it, I would be fine. I could become "a good girl" again. And if I was a good girl, my parents wouldn't fight, my mother would be happy, and I could sit in sunshine without fear. I didn't realize then that the narrative of being a good girl meant I had to stay silent. That I had to learn to deny what lay under the surface so I could maintain the lies on top.

But I knew what lay beneath those waters. I knew that the calmest, most tranquil waters could belie danger, darkness underneath. I knew that I'd never see the crocodile just under the surface. Whenever I see flamingos now, I cannot help but see blood on their bodies.

Chapter 4
No Act of Kindness

Cierra Rodriguez was rude to me.

I shouldn't have taken it personally. She was rude to everyone. Except Dr. James Oleske. I had never seen any of his patients being rude to him. Not because his patients were mostly children, but because Dr. Oleske had that ineffable quality that softened even rude, brooding teenagers. Some people would call that "saintliness," but it was really a depth of kindness even fourteen-year-old Cierra found impossible to defend against.

I knocked on her door and entered before she could answer. She hinged forward in her hospital bed, stiffened her spine, and turned her back on me. It was morning, but the room was in shadow, the blinds on the windows tightly drawn, the fluorescent lights turned off.

I sighed without making a sound. "Good morning, Cierra."

She refused to answer.

"I need to listen to your heart and lungs, okay?" I cajoled.

She refused to move.

I walked to her bed with purpose but hesitated in touching her. She pounced. "Get out of my room!"

"Listen, Cierra, I need to examine you. I'm supposed to be your doctor." I tried to say this with authority, as though I were not a lowly medical student. But my voice sounded uncertain.

Again she screamed, "Get out of my room!"

"But I—"

"Get out!"

I left the room. And despite the fact that she was only a child, a child infected with HIV, I did not like Cierra Rodriguez.

Until late one night, several months later.

It was two o'clock in the morning, and I was a fourth-year medical student on call as an acting intern in pediatrics. In the midst of writing my admission note for a six-month-old infant devastated by diarrhea and dehydration, another casualty of rotavirus, I was startled when a fellow medical student slipped into the seat next to me.

"Jerry, what are you doing here?"

His gaunt face, a mop of dark hair falling into his eyes, bore signs of protracted weeping.

"Are you okay?"

He did not respond. Jerry was often ridiculed as the class clown. He was usually smiling or telling a joke, good-natured about his classmates' merciless teasing.

"What's the matter?"

"Cierra is dying and I—" He squeezed his eyes shut, even as more tears poured out.

I handed him the box of tissues that was sitting on the counter. The nursing station was empty, the nurses gone to check vital signs ordered on their patients. And the unit clerk, normally taking down orders from patient charts or filing paperwork, was away on an errand. Caught in a pool of light, I waited for Jerry to stop crying.

"It's okay, it's okay." I offered platitudes against his sorrow.

"Cierra is dying and there's nothing I can do about it. She's only fourteen years old." Tears cascaded down his cheeks.

"I know, Jerry, I know."

Cierra had full-blown AIDS. Her HIV status became known when she was hospitalized with her first episode of pneumonia and failed to improve on conventional antibiotics. She had been in the pediatric intensive care unit, on a ventilator, requiring oxygen and a breathing tube. Dr. Oleske took over her care when cultures of the saline washes taken from her lungs grew out *Pneumocystis carinii*. Cierra had PCP. She recovered from her first bout of PCP only to be hospitalized repeatedly for recurrent pneumonia, progressive weight loss, and severe malnutrition. Now she was dying.

Jerry looked at me. "Do you know what Cierra did the first time I met her?"

I shook my head.

"She screamed at me to get out of her room."

"She yelled at me too," I said.

"But I wouldn't leave. I just kept talking. She tried to ignore me. I came into her room every day—I told her I grew on people." A mischievous grin appeared, a trace of the old Jerry. "One day, she started talking back. When I least expected it. You know something? I like teenagers."

"I can't stand teenagers," I said. "They have no respect, and they mouth off on you all the time."

"That's because you're Korean. You were raised to respect your elders and all that. I bet you never talked back to your parents—I argued with mine all the time," Jerry said.

"I *never* argued with my parents," I said, my face set in prim lines. At the time, I took pride in being stereotyped as "Korean," a model minority, an example to emulate. And when I was young, the very idea of dissenting from my parents was unfathomable. I saw what happened to my older sister Susan when she disobeyed—a beating.

Jerry laughed. "Then I'm sure Cierra came as a shock to you. She's twice as belligerent as any teenager I've ever met. A tough nut. But then, she had to be. It's the only way she survived."

"How do you know all this?"

"I met Cierra last year. I visit when she's in the hospital." Jerry became very still. "Do you know how she got AIDS?"

I shook my head.

"She was raped by her father."

My head snapped back.

"The bastard had HIV. Her little brother was diagnosed as a baby. Then her mother got tested. Cierra didn't get tested for years—she never told anyone about the abuse. When her mom died, she wouldn't let DYFS place her brother anywhere without her. He died a couple of months ago."

I stared at the Formica table, my body rigid. *Don't cry, don't cry, don't cry.*

I reacted viscerally to the knowledge that Cierra had been sexually assaulted. During my medical career, that's the way I would react every time I heard yet another story of a child having been sexually abused. My body seized; my breath trapped. Terror flooded me like when I was nine years old. I didn't know then that my body remembered the trauma while my mind rejected it.

"That's when she stopped fighting," Jerry said. "She'd sworn to me that she was going to outlive her father—or as she calls him, 'that sono-fabitch.' It gave her such satisfaction, knowing that he was dying in some crack house. But after her brother died, she gave up."

❧

I heard about Dr. James Oleske long before I ever met him. Newspaper articles anointed him a saint for treating babies and children with AIDS. A princess from a tiny Eastern European principality donated more than a hundred thousand dollars specifically for Dr. Oleske's pediatric AIDS research. A foster mother took her adopted child infected with HIV on a twenty-nine-hour train ride from New Orleans to Newark, so he could be treated by Dr. Oleske. She had seen the same made-for-TV movie I had about his life and work: *The Littlest Victims*. The actor Tim Matheson played Jim Oleske. I assumed they looked alike.

When I finally met Dr. Oleske, in my third year of medical school, I was surprised by his physical appearance: a rotund, Santa-like figure with a matching shock of white hair, despite his middle, not old, age. He lacked a beard but wore boxy black-framed glasses. And he had the kindest eyes I have ever encountered. I thought it was serendipity that Dr. Oleske was my attending physician while I was on a pediatric rotation in my third year of medical school, the time when most students choose their specialties. I see now that it was fate.

In the early years of the AIDS epidemic, children were most commonly infected through the placenta, from mother to baby. There was no cure for HIV and a dearth of treatment options. When Jim Oleske first suggested that transplacental transmission of HIV was the cause of so much suffering in so many children, scientists, including those at the National Institutes of Health, the most respected body of researchers in the US, basically told him he was crazy. HIV/AIDS was such a stigmatizing disease. In those first years of the epidemic, to suggest that children were getting what was considered a plague upon homosexuals and drug addicts was tantamount to blasphemy. It almost ruined Dr. Oleske's career.

Yet he told me the story without bitterness: "They said I should leave it alone. More than one person hinted that if I persisted, my career would be over." But Jim Oleske would not let it go. Carefully, he amassed the data he needed to support his theory and published it. He pioneered pediatric AIDS research and treatment without regard to political agenda or public prejudice.

Jim Oleske is the kind of doctor who, despite his fame during the peak of the AIDS epidemic in this country, had a simple nameplate on his door, indistinguishable from any other in the maze of offices at University Hospital. The only adornment on its blue-gray surface was the black silhouette of a tree on a white piece of paper, with words attributed to Aesop: "No act of kindness, no matter how small, is ever wasted." At first I thought it was trite. But after I got to know Dr. Oleske, I saw how much he believed in those words. How true they were.

In July 1991, as a fourth-year medical student, I chose to take an elective in pediatric infectious diseases with Dr. Oleske. I worked closely with him and Maria, a congenial but no-nonsense second-year pediatric resident, on the infectious disease service. We rounded every day on the service, including weekends. It seemed to me that half of all children admitted to Children's Hospital that year were infected with HIV. Like seven-year-old Carlos and ten-year-old Innocensio, brothers with hemophilia and also HIV because of tainted blood. Like six-month-old Tamar, with PCP and AIDS, who struggled under her plastic oxygen tent, her ribs and neck muscles tugging and pulling with each excruciating breath.

Despite the horrifying nature of the infectious disease service, it was not all grim on rounds. Dr. Oleske often made us laugh with stories about his life and his patients. "When I was a pediatric infectious disease fellow at Emory, I thought I was pretty smart," he started one such story. "I was consulted on a child with lesions all over his body. These bumps had just started, and the nurses wanted to know if he had chicken pox and should he be quarantined. I examined him and declared the rash to be molluscum contagiosum. Everyone was impressed." He paused with a smile. "The next day, his lesions became vesicular and started weeping—it was chicken pox. Those nurses were so mad at me."

Dr. Oleske told another story about a patient of his, a teenager with AIDS. Etienne had recovered from PCP but struggled with malabsorption and a lack of appetite because of a gastrointestinal motility disorder. He was transferred to a chronic-care facility to manage his malnutrition, to prevent him from wasting away. "I would visit him every week and bring him a Taylor Ham, egg, and cheese sandwich—my favorite. I would eat mine in a few bites. He would take over an *hour* to eat his. Every bite was painful to watch." Dr. Oleske smiled. The image of Dr. Oleske sneaking peeks at his pager, holding in his sighs, made me laugh. And the image of Etienne and Dr. Oleske sitting together made me want to cry.

Once, I asked Dr. Oleske to tell me the story behind the movie about his life.

"When they first asked me to do it, I turned it down," he said.

"But why?" I asked.

He was modest in his reply. "I didn't think it was appropriate. I didn't know how my wife and children would feel about it."

"What changed your mind?"

"They offered to fund a social worker for our HIV clinic. I couldn't turn that down."

∽

A few months before I graduated from medical school in 1992, I attended a lecture Dr. Oleske gave on his HIV/AIDS research. One of the slides he flashed on the screen was a picture of his desk with stacks of papers piled several feet high. He told the audience that those were grants he and his team had written that were not funded by the NIH. I marveled at Dr. Oleske's persistence. I would have given up long ago.

Dr. Oleske was a truly remarkable person. Despite all the obstacles, he toiled relentlessly on behalf of children infected with HIV and dying of AIDS. And he did it with such patience and kindness. He did not allow sorrow to curdle into despair or bitterness. He did everything in his power to help those children, and he refused to give up. But he allowed himself to revel in the small victories—the gain of half a pound by a child who had steadily been losing weight; fevers decreasing in a child who had spiked temperatures so high that sweat had matted her hair and beaded her upper lip; the disappearance of thrush in the mouth of a child whose tongue had been coated with white plaques. He knew these tiny changes indicated progress—small and excruciating but, still, audacious and triumphant. He knew that part of being a doctor was not necessarily to treat or to cure. Sometimes it was our duty to bear witness to the lives of our patients, to have them know their lives mattered. And he knew that sometimes our patients teach us invaluable lessons about our own lives.

That was the case with me and Cierra Rodriguez. Even as I refused to acknowledge what happened to me as a child, I instinctively felt deep admiration for Cierra and her courage—howling and thrashing, refusing to stay silent, unleashing her pain and sorrow for the violence done to her body. Her rage was a radical act of self-preservation. She didn't care that she was not "a good girl."

The only person remaining whose opinion Cierra cared about was Dr. Oleske. On rounds with residents and medical students, when he would enter her room, she didn't pretend she was sleeping. She ignored the rest of us, but she smiled at Dr. Oleske, eager for his approval. He joked with her, listened to her story, bore witness to her pain. He made her feel less lonely in the world. And now I can see myself in Cierra and how she blossomed around him. He was the perfect father figure for lost girls. On pediatric rounds, Dr. Oleske praised my patient assessments, my treatment plans. I basked in the glow of his approval. I felt like I could be a good doctor, that I hadn't made a mistake going to medical school.

Dr. Oleske maintained balance. He laughed and encouraged everyone around him to find humor, even though life seemed unbearable. He was often pensive about going to yet another burial of yet another child who had died of AIDS. But he was also gentle and generous with the people who knew those children. He frequently talked about how much solace a funeral service provided those who attended it. Beauty and joy occupied the same sphere as sorrow and grief.

That day in 1992, Dr. Oleske finished his lecture with a story.

He faced the audience in his suit and black-framed glasses, hands in his pockets.

"A terrible storm has passed, and thousands of starfish have washed onto shore. A man walks along the waterline. He picks up a starfish and throws it back into the ocean. And he keeps doing this, over and over. A young girl is watching. She asks the man, 'Why are you doing this? You can't save them all. What you're doing doesn't matter.'"

Jim Oleske paused for a moment.

"The man picks up another starfish and throws it back into the ocean. He says to the young girl, 'It matters to this starfish.'"

I still think about the allegory Dr. Oleske told that day. At the time, I thought he was talking about his work. I thought he was saying that the storm of AIDS had hit, and the children with HIV, like the starfish, were vulnerable, and it was our duty as doctors to try and do everything we could to save them. And, by extension, I thought he was making a metaphor about every patient being a starfish. We can't help or change the lives of all of our patients, but we have to try. Because every act of kindness matters.

Now I think differently. Now I think that story means so much more. I think it is about what we are faced with in the aftermath of a storm, any storm, in our lives. All we can do is pick up and go on.

I became a pediatrician because of Dr. Oleske. Young and idealistic, I thought that in order to be a good doctor, I had to be a "saint" like him. I had no hope of measuring up. There are not many people in the world like Jim Oleske. But the lessons he tried to teach me, about courage and kindness, I could have learned. I could have tried to maintain balance and perspective. Instead I became disillusioned by what disease and the indifference of society had done to children. I could not accept how much I wanted to help them and yet how powerless I was in the face of limited and shrinking resources—no one cared about poor, sick, dying children in inner-city neighborhoods.

As the years passed, I was also afraid that I had disappointed Dr. Oleske. I was supposed to complete my general pediatric residency and then return to Newark to do my fellowship with him in allergy, immunology, and infectious diseases. I was supposed to join his team and help children with HIV/AIDS. Instead I got married, had children, and became a general pediatrician, not an infectious disease expert in HIV. As time went on, I went from working full-time to part-time, and then I stopped practicing altogether. During those years, I composed several letters to Dr. Oleske, justifying my choices. I never sent those letters. I did not think he would censure me, but I thought he would be deeply disappointed.

Increasingly, I doubt this version. A man like Jim Oleske, who believed so profoundly in the power of kindness, would not be judgmental. Instead of calling me a failure, he would probably ask if writing brought me joy. He would understand that life sometimes takes us places, and we don't know where we're going until we get there. I wish I had listened to Dr. Oleske and the lessons of love and courage he was trying to teach me all those years ago.

And I wish I could go back to the night with Jerry as Cierra lay dying. I wish I had gone into her room as her breaths slowed. I want to tell her that it's okay to leave this world, to reunite with her mother and brother. A fierce warrior sometimes needs to rest. I want to believe that Cierra lifted out of her diseased and ravaged body and walked out the door.

Chapter 5
Loss of Breath

At Children's Hospital there was a ritual that was dreaded and yet welcomed every year around the Christmas holidays. In exchange for having either Christmas or New Year's off, the residents worked a brutal schedule during the holiday they *weren't* taking off—twenty-four hours on, twenty-four hours off. But in reality it was more like twenty-six or twenty-seven hours without sleep, then barely time to stagger home, shower, eat, sleep a few hours, and be back at the hospital again for another marathon session of work. Constant fluorescent lighting befuddled our perceptions of day and night, not that it mattered when we were mostly working in rooms without natural light. Since half the residents were given days off during one holiday or the other, the other half were split between the twenty-four-on, twenty-four-off schedule. Only a quarter of the residents usually working at the hospital were physically present during the holidays. A skeleton crew of physicians.

Ironically, the holidays usually brought a tidal wave of admissions to Children's Hospital. One year, a fellow third-year resident and I set the hospital record for the most admissions in one night. Between our two teams of four first-years and two supervising residents, we admitted sixty children into the hospital the day after Christmas. I don't think that record has been broken. All day and night I ran from one hospital room to another, from the pediatric floors to the ER and back, from one nursing station to another, from one treatment room to another, and back yet again to another hospital room and another sick child. I sat in the cafeteria the next morning so depleted I couldn't move, wondering if I could stay awake for the drive home.

The year I was an intern, a first-year resident barely managing to keep afloat in the exhaustion and demands of being a doctor, the holiday schedule almost broke me. I sat on the floor of the treatment room in one of the general pediatric wards, my back against the treatment table, my knees bent, my elbows braced, my head in my hands, unable to stop sobbing. I had tried to place an IV in an infant who needed fluids. And I failed. I had stuck the child with so many needles he resembled a pincushion, red dots all over his arms and legs, his skin starting to bruise. His nurse was about to take him back to his room, and I was supposed to clean up the mess I had made. Needles, gauze, syringes, tape all lay in waste, glaring reminders of my failure. It started with one teardrop. One minute I was standing, and the next I was on the floor. Mucus and tears oozed between my fingers, even as I pressed both palms over my mouth, muffling a tide of snorting, gulping, wheezing. Both the nurse and the medical student left the room. *I hate this,* I thought. *I'm no good at being a doctor.* I wanted to walk out the door of the hospital and never come back. But I had student loan debt, tens of thousands of dollars. And what else could I do? Medical school only prepared me to be a doctor. Nothing else.

My parents had told my sisters and me that we'd come to America so that we would have opportunities girls did not have in Korea. But as a foreign medical graduate, my father had to repeat his residency. First he had to take the ECFMGs, the exams given by the Educational Commission for Foreign Medical Graduates, in order to be eligible for a residency. The exams were intentionally written to be more difficult to pass than the national boards given to American medical graduates, but it took my father only two years to pass, when most of his peers took much longer or never passed. At the age of forty-three, my father took on hundred-hour workweeks as a resident in a New York hospital. The six of us moved into a two-bedroom apartment in a building populated by working-class Latino immigrants, near the Lincoln Tunnel in New Jersey. I could see the Empire State Building across the Hudson River from the bedroom I shared with my three sisters. For college I went to pharmacy school, like a dutiful daughter, because my father was adamant that pharmacology and organic chemistry was excellent preparation for medical school. I secretly took Shakespeare classes and Eighteenth-Century British Novel, and sometimes I allowed myself to dream about getting my PhD in English literature.

Although I had two older sisters, I became the physician in the family. I call myself "the idiot who listened." My father, bereft of sons, insisted that one of his four girls had to become a doctor.

The day I got into medical school was one of the rare times my mother physically touched me. Her stout arms reached up to hug me, her diminutive feet in high heels. The soft flesh of her cheek pressed into my neck, her Estée Lauder perfume lingering in my nose.

"You are beautiful and smart."

Although she rarely told me that I was intelligent, she rewarded my excellence in school by letting me buy books or candy or roller skates. But she had never before said that I was beautiful. That same day, after a celebratory dinner at an expensive restaurant, as we walked to the parking lot, my father said that he was proud of me. I was startled by his praise, since he had always been quick to find fault with my actions. Smiling, his face flushed from drinking, he reached out to pat me on the back. My father, like my mother, had not been physically demonstrative. I was unprepared for his sudden touch. I will never forget the warmth of his long, thin fingers pressing into my shoulder.

Whenever I desperately wanted to quit medical school—which was often, especially during dissection of the human brain in Gross Anatomy, where we had to slit open the skulls of our cadavers with a

Stryker saw—the way my parents looked at me that day stopped me. I could not be the jangsohn they had desperately prayed for, but I could become the doctor they wished me to be. I had to force myself not to throw up every single time the acrid smell of burning bone against sharp rotating steel assaulted my nasal passages. Every single time I stepped into the stainless-steel-clad lab filled with cadavers, the odor of formaldehyde and rotting flesh elicited my gag reflex. But I finished medical school.

"Are you okay?" Olivia, my senior resident, pushed open the door of the treatment room. She closed it behind her.

I shook my head. Mouth open, chest heaving, I still could not get enough air into my lungs.

"What's wrong?" she said as she looked down at me.

"I can't do this anymore," I said, my words slurring as I hiccupped, gasped, and grunted.

"Come on, it's not the first time you couldn't get an IV. And it's not going to be the last. You're tired. You're at your wit's end—I've been there. But you need to get up."

I couldn't look at her. My body shook uncontrollably, and even with my head bowed I couldn't see the linoleum floor through the wall of tears.

Olivia sat down next to me. "I know it's hard. It's actually fucking hard." She blew out her breath. "But we have to keep going because these kids need us," she said, her voice low and urgent.

I knew she expected me to bounce up and carry on. But even the guilt wasn't enough. I had come undone.

"Stop crying and get up." She stood up and pulled on my shoulder, tugging at my arm.

I followed with the rest of my body. I hunched over the treatment table, my elbows and hands pushing into the soft vinyl, my sobs gradually slowing. I looked at Olivia, her blue scrubs blurred through the sticky, salty liquid clinging to my eyelashes.

Her facial expression was not unkind, but not sympathetic. "You can't do that again. The nurse saw you. The medical student saw you. They're going to talk. You're going to be seen as a weak resident. You don't want that. You need to act strong and confident."

I never forgot what Olivia said. I was so ashamed of my loss of control, revealing vulnerability that would surely be used against me, that I resolved to encase myself in an armor of indifference. It was pretense but I thought it would protect me. After all, I was raised by a woman who abhorred crying—whenever my sisters or I cried, she mocked us for acting like babies. My mother rarely cried. And when she did, afterward she pretended it had never happened.

My father did not tolerate crying either. When I was a sophomore in high school, I came home agitated one afternoon because the school nurse had said I had scoliosis of the spine. Worried that something was wrong with me, I waited in excruciating agony for my father to come home that night. After he examined me, he dismissed the nurse's opinion and told me I was fine. I burst into tears. He looked at me with disdain. *"Why are you so stupid?"*

A year after my treatment-room meltdown, I rocked back on my heels, my arms crossed over my blue scrubs, my mouth slightly agape. I stared intently at the monitor as the numbers slowly continued to decrease and flashed in warning. The alarm dinged furiously without end. The boy's heart was in failure, as was the rest of his body, his organs shutting down one by one: his kidneys not making urine, his liver enzymes escalating beyond measure, his lungs less pliable on the ventilator. And now his heart rate was dropping despite all the drugs we were injecting. I lost count of how many times his heart stopped and how many times we restarted it. A wayward strep infection gone rogue, and now he was in the PICU, his body in multisystem organ failure. This seven-year-old was dying.

I stared at the monitor, waiting to see something change. Nothing. I leaned against the wall of the isolation room, let my head drop, and closed my eyes. When I opened my eyes again, I saw Dr. Murray crying. As the attending physician of record, she had come in when the boy first arrested about an hour before. Now it seemed like an eternity ago. As the second-year resident on call in the PICU that night, I was supposed to be running the "code," the resuscitation effort.

"He's on an epi drip. We've given him norepi. And bretylium. What else should we do?" I asked Dr. Murray. Bretylium is a drug of last resort.

"We need to stop," she said, tears running down her face unchecked.

I said nothing in response.

"We have to stop," she said. She didn't brush the tears away, made no attempt to hide the fact that she was crying.

I avoided looking at her. I was so disconcerted that an attending physician was crying. Her behavior seemed like a breach of protocol. I remembered what Olivia had said, that people would talk. Attending physicians were supposed to exude confidence. And in chaotic situations, they remained calm and centered. Why was she crying?

We watched as the monitor read "0." The number blinking over and over and over. The PICU night nurses crowded the entrance of the isolation room. The respiratory therapist and the code team of residents stood around, stunned.

Dr. Murray turned to face us. "Thank you for everything you've done. There's nothing more we can do. He needs his parents now." She was still crying as she left the room.

When his parents entered the PICU, everyone retreated. I could hear his mother's keening from the nursing station.

"Are you okay?" one of the nurses asked me, her eyes puffy and red.

I saw some of the nurses standing together, talking softly, reaching out to touch each other on the shoulder, arm, back. Occasionally, one of them would draw up her hand and wipe away her tears. These nurses hadn't been in the room as that boy was dying. Why were they crying?

"I'm fine," I answered.

The death certificate needed to be filled out, the exact time of death to be verified. All the notes documenting what had happened still needed to be written. I sat at the white Formica counter, my head bent over the metal binding of the boy's chart, gripping my pen.

Once when I was ten years old, my mother broke down crying. She told me that she had failed as a woman because she had no sons. Only daughters. She was overwhelmed by her shame. I never witnessed my mother weep with such heartbreak again.

I was in medical school when I saw my father cry for the first and only time. My sisters and I were visiting him at a minimum-security federal penitentiary, where he was serving eighteen months for Medicaid fraud. In the barren visitor's room, my father, in an orange jumpsuit, had picked up the black phone on the other side of the smeared glass. But he was crying so hard he couldn't speak. I can still see him—his hand covering his eyes, his shoulders shaking, his mouth gasping for air.

When I think about that night in the PICU, what is burned into my mind's eye is the image of the boy in his hospital bed, his thin body immobile, the monitor showing his ever-slowing heart rhythm, the acceleration of numbers to a blinking "0," and Dr. Murray's face glistening with wetness. And yet she did nothing to hide it, as though she were glad she was crying. Because that is a sign of grieving. And grief cannot be deferred or buried without exacting a catastrophic cost.

Chapter 6
A Shard of Glass

The air squeezed out of my lungs as I read the first page: "Steven Koon, Plaintiff, versus Helena Rho and Children's Hospital, Defendants." The papers scattered onto my lap.

In my third and final year of training, I was sitting in the small resident's room in continuity clinic. While waiting for a patient's lab results, I was slogging through two weeks of mail that had accumulated during my honeymoon. Usually the things that were stuffed in a resident's mailbox were weekly hospital bulletins announcing upcoming grand rounds, pink slips from patients' families asking for return phone calls, reminders from Medical Records to finish dictating discharge summaries. Not a malpractice lawsuit.

I turned the pages of the complaint, my hands shaking. Fragments of sentences caught my attention, only for my eyes to skip to the next line with no understanding of the words I had just read. *Oh my god, oh my god, oh my god* were the only words looping in my head.

This is what I remember: "Betty Koon, mother and guardian of Steven Koon, alleges the Defendants, Helena Rho and Children's Hospital, are responsible for grave harm to the Plaintiff . . . a punitive award for pain and suffering is demanded in the amount of $100,000 . . ."

Who was this boy? What had I done?

I clutched my head between my hands, my elbows on the Formica counter. My stomach clenched so hard I thought I was going to vomit.

Another resident entered the room. "Helena, what's wrong?"

"What?" I turned to look at her, my focus blurred.

"What's wrong?" Her words sounded loud and urgent.

"I got sued." I heard the disbelief in my voice.

"Holy shit."

Silence ensued.

"You better go see Louise in Legal. I'll let Dr. Chan know where you are."

"I'm in the middle of seeing a patient," I protested.

"I'll take care of it. Just go."

∾

Louise sat at her large mahogany desk and read through the complaint. She arched her blond eyebrows at me. "Before we go any further, my advice is that you don't speak to anyone about this. Except to me and your attorney. What you say to us is privileged."

"What?"

"The opposing side could use your words against you," she said.

"How?" I remained bewildered.

"Say you're talking to your husband about this case, and you say something like, 'It was my fault.' At your deposition, the opposing counsel could ask, 'Did you talk to anyone about this case?' And because you're a good person, you say, 'Yes.' Now you're screwed. Because now he's going to make you say that you thought it was your fault." Louise tipped her head from side to side, her body like a metronome, keeping time to her words.

"You could lie." She paused. "But it's better for you not to talk about it. Not with the other residents. Not with the attendings. No one."

I was supposed to keep what was happening to me a secret? Not that I was in any rush to tell people that I was being sued. Even then, I knew my husband was not someone I could lean on. And I was used to keeping secrets, staying silent.

"Speaking of the case, do you remember this boy?" she asked.

I felt like an idiot. "No. It sounds terrible, but I saw so many patients in the ER."

Louise picked up the phone. "Let's get the chart from Medical Records and refresh your memory."

My own handwriting documented the events, which occurred two years earlier, when I was a first-year resident. In the medical chart, there was even a crude drawing I did of the boy's hand. As I read through the chart, what happened that night came flooding back.

It had been another busy Saturday night in the ER. Charts of patients yet to be seen were stacking up. The night nurses were riding the residents to hurry up. I picked up a chart with the chief complaint "laceration of hand" scrawled across the top. When I entered the exam room, I saw a little boy, a towhead with blue eyes, sitting on his mother's lap. He was seven years old.

"Hi, I'm Dr. Rho. How're you doing tonight?" I tried to sound cheerful, a smile on my face.

The mother just stared at me, her blue eyes blank.

"What brings you to the hospital?" I tried again.

"I want to see the doctor. Not the nurse." Her eyes swept over me in a scornful flicker.

"I *am* the doctor," I said, my voice quiet but firm.

Being female, small, and Asian, I was frequently mistaken for a nurse instead of a doctor. When caught in their error, most parents either apologized or, at least, acknowledged their mistake. This mother craned her neck to look past me, still searching for her real doctor.

"We're very busy tonight. There's going to be a long wait to see another doctor," I warned.

"I'm not waiting anymore." Sharp creases pulled down the corners of her mouth. "You'll have to do."

I bit my tongue and refrained from sarcastically saying, *Thank you.*

"What brings you to the ER tonight?" I said instead.

"He cut his hand." She turned the boy's palm up, revealing dried and still-oozing blood from numerous scratches and cuts, along with black smudges of dirt and gravel.

"What happened?" I stepped closer to examine the mess.

The blond boy, who had eyed me with suspicion as soon as I entered, now started to scream.

"I'm not going to hurt you," I assured him.

He screamed louder.

His mother raised her voice. "He was running around the playground and fell."

He tried to jerk his hand away, but I kept a firm grasp. "Is that glass?" I wondered aloud, as light glinted off a foreign body in his hand.

"Yeah. There were a whole bunch of broken bottles laying around. But I couldn't see too good in the dark," she said.

Broken bottles? What was a seven-year-old doing in a dark place like that so late at night?

When I approached the boy with a large saline-filled syringe, to cleanse his hand, he thrashed himself off his mother's lap and howled on the floor. I reached out to pick him up. He kicked me. I told his mother that we needed help and stepped out of the room. For a moment, all I could hear was ringing in my ears.

Immobilized in a "papoose" with large Velcro straps across his forehead, chest, abdomen, and legs, his blond hair damp with struggle, the boy continued screaming. I was certain I would be deaf by the time this ordeal was over. I asked his mother to help me keep his hand still.

"I can't," she said, her eyes shifting away. She pushed back her long, stringy hair with trembling fingers and hunched forward with her arms crossed, scratching her skin. She seemed high to me, her eyes rimmed red, her hands fidgety.

"Please, try not to move your hand. It'll be over soon," I implored the boy in vain.

He kept howling.

During my repeated attempts to rinse his hand while he was jerking it away, the boy upturned the washbasin, water flying into the air. My hair, my face, my clothes became soaked. Needing a reprieve, I sent him for x-rays of his hand. I put his x-rays on a light board and found one of the ER attending physicians to look at them with me. Several foreign bodies were still lodged in the soft tissue, but there was no fracture. The attending said, "Try to get out as much as you can. A foreign body won't cause an infection, but it can be uncomfortable for the patient."

I tried to follow his advice. Despite the little boy screeching mercilessly in my ear, I doggedly kept removing gravel and glass from his hand. I sent him for a repeat x-ray, which I viewed with the ER attending again. I saw a piece of glass near his middle finger. I went back and probed and rinsed his hand again and again, his twitching, squirming, and screaming all maddening distractions. I thought the glass was gone.

The boy had several cuts, but only one, near his wrist, was deep and long enough to require stitches. I approximated the skin edges cleanly and placed all five sutures in a close and regular pattern so he would not have a scar when he grew up. I enjoyed stitching skin, and I was technically proficient. By the time I finished, the boy was snoring in exhaustion.

I instructed his mother in wound care: Clean his stitches with soapy water, dry with gauze, and cover with antibiotic ointment. Change the bandage twice a day, look for redness or swelling or pus, and come back to the hospital immediately if any of those signs of infection surfaced. The stitches could be removed in ten to fourteen days, depending on the rate of healing.

The last thing I said to her: "Keep the stitches clean and dry."

In Louise's office, I stared at my signature at the bottom of the emergency room chart. I flipped the page and read the addendum. The radiologist who reviewed the images of the boy's hand had notified the ER that, on repeat x-ray, there was still a piece of glass lodged near his middle finger, but no documentation that it had been removed. There were several phone calls and messages left at the boy's home, but no call back from his mother.

Three days later, the boy returned to the ER. The resident who saw him noted that the bandage over the stitches was dirty and had not been changed since the boy's initial visit. His hand was swollen, pus extruding from the stitches, and he was admitted for IV antibiotics to prevent compartment syndrome, a dangerous compromise to the use of his hand. In a different part of his hand, the piece of glass that I had missed was removed. He had an uneventful forty-eight-hour stay and was discharged to home.

I exhaled with a loud whoosh and closed my eyes. *Thank God.*

"As you can see, he's fine," Louise said.

"I screwed up." I put my head in my hands, hunching my shoulders.

"You made a mistake. Stop being so hard on yourself," she admonished.

"A good doctor doesn't make mistakes." My hands squeezed against my temples.

"So, this makes you a bad doctor?" she demanded.

"Yes," I said.

"Who do you know that doesn't make any mistakes?" she said.

"All the doctors I know," I said, crossing my arms, sitting rigidly in my chair.

"Name one," she challenged.

"Ira Rubinstein," I said without hesitation.

Ira was one of the most meticulous doctors I had ever known. Long after the other attendings had gone home, Ira would agonize over why a patient's creatinine level had gone from 0.4 to 0.5, both values within the normal range. He would run his hands through his salt-and-pepper hair, muttering, "Why? Why did it change?"

"Ira's been sued," Louise said.

"What?"

"One of his patients had a severe reaction. Not Ira's fault. But she died, and her father sued. I advised Ira to fight it. But he didn't have the stomach for a trial, so we settled the suit."

"That's horrible. But that's a bad outcome, not a mistake," I said.

"Don't kid yourself. Ira's made mistakes," Louise said dismissively. "Who else?"

"I don't know."

Louise locked her eyes onto mine. "What if I told you John Ainsley had been sued?"

I was too stunned to speak. Louise was talking about one of the most respected pediatric attending physicians at Children's Hospital. Dr. Ainsley literally wrote the book on pediatrics. When he was my attending in continuity clinic, I presented to him a patient with short stature. He asked me if the child had triangular facies and frontal bossing, a prominent forehead. He also asked me if the boy had a small penis. Without seeing or examining my patient, Dr. Ainsley correctly diagnosed him with pituitary dwarfism, a diagnosis confirmed by the pediatric endocrinologist.

"John was the attending when a baby was admitted to rule out sepsis. They did the spinal tap and started the baby on antibiotics. But it was too late. He had meningitis and died. The mother sued. I told John that we should settle, but he wanted to go to trial." Louise tapped her pen against her desk. "Juries are notorious for giving big awards when they want to punish doctors. And they thought John was condescending. A know-it-all. They punished him."

Louise tilted her head slowly to the side. "John gave up direct clinical care after that case. I don't think it ruined his life. But it changed him."

These physicians I admired had been sued. Like me. But I thought they were victims of circumstance, bad outcomes and bad juries. Not bad doctoring. It was inescapable: I had left a piece of glass in a child's hand.

⤲

In April 1983, I was seventeen years old, in my senior year of high school. Admission letters were arriving at the homes of thousands of college hopefuls, but not mine. The days went by and I received nothing.

I was home on one of those nonspecific school holidays, like a "clerical day," and the mail had just been delivered. My mother called down from her bedroom and asked if I had gotten an acceptance letter. No, I answered. Still nothing. I went to the family room and turned on the TV, hoping to catch the last of the soaps for the afternoon.

My mother materialized in the archway. *"Why haven't you gotten your acceptance to Harvard?"* she demanded. My mother spoke to me in Korean because it was easier for her.

"Mom, I don't want to go to Harvard," I answered in English because it was easier for me.

I wanted to go to Yale. I had visited with my friend Terry, and to me, a first-generation immigrant who was desperate to belong, Yale's history and gothic architecture with ivy on the walls all blared status and acceptance.

My mother dismissed what I said with a shake of her head. *"You're going to Harvard,"* she said with certainty.

I didn't argue. It would be pointless.

"You have to call them," she announced.

"What? Call Harvard?"

"They should have sent their acceptance by now." She paced back and forth.

"Who cares if they forgot to send a rejection letter?" I said with a defiance I did not feel.

"Call them right now," she demanded.

"Mom, please, it's going to look lame."

She grabbed my arm and pulled me to the gold-and-ivory Princess phone in the foyer.

I made the call.

"I'm sorry, Miss Rho, Harvard was unable to offer you admission. My sincere apologies for the lost letter," said the nice woman on the phone.

"Thank you," I said. My face burned with shame. I set my lips in a thin line to stop them from quivering. "I told you they were going to reject me."

"This is a catastrophe! How did this happen?" my mother said, her hands on the sides of her face, her head whipping back and forth.

"I didn't want to go to Harvard anyway. I'm going to Yale," I said, my arms crossed.

Yale University's minority program had tried to recruit me. But my parents scoffed at the offer. They said I should be able to get in on my own merit, that I wasn't a charity case. I attended an inner-city high school with other immigrant children whose first language was not English, but my parents insisted it was a level playing field. And I believed them. I applied to Yale under the regular admissions process. I was sure they were going to accept me.

I talked to my friends about visiting them at Georgetown and Princeton when I was at Yale. Not, *if* I was at Yale. In my mind, I had already moved into one of those residential colleges on Yale's campus. I pictured myself eating lunch at one of the dining halls, surrounded by old stone and dark wood, sunlight slanting through leaded-glass windows.

"*This is a catastrophe! This is a catastrophe!*" My mother was now pacing the room.

"Mom, please stop."

Suddenly she turned and ran up the stairs. I was relieved she had stopped belaboring the moment. But my reprieve was short-lived. She came back down and thrust two thin envelopes at me, the sharp edges pointed at my chest.

I flinched. I saw the elaborate crests of Princeton and Yale.

"How long have you had these?" I asked.

"*It doesn't matter. You're not going to Harvard,*" my mother said. "*How could you let this happen? You didn't try hard enough.*" She spun away from me, stormed up the stairs to her bedroom, and slammed the door.

I stood in the foyer, wishing that I could change what had happened. That I could go back to the moment before I called Harvard, before my body felt like it had burst into flames, scorched and seared. I looked up at my mother's bedroom door, wondering if I should plead with her to forgive me. But I knew it would be no use.

I walked out of the house into pouring rain. I pulled up the hood of my black sweatshirt, hunched my shoulders, and kept walking. *This is a catastrophe.* My parents had insisted that I apply only to Harvard, Yale, and Princeton. Although my two older sisters had failed to get into those schools, my parents were certain it would be different with me—I was going to be the valedictorian of my class; I had been ranked number one for four years; I played the piano.

Koreans have a name for this kind of child, the one that other children envy, the one they are told to emulate: *umchin tdal.* The child that other children despise. I did not know it then, but my sisters hated me. They called me "the chosen one." Our mother constantly told them that they should be more like me, smarter and taller. As if they had any control over their height.

As I walked through the steady rain, I thought about going until I could not take one more step. But water soaked through my sweatshirt. I was shaking from the chill. I stopped on a bridge where a creek flowed underneath. I thought about leaping. But even with the heavy rain, the creek was a meager trickle. I knew I would only break my legs on the jagged rocks. Still, I wanted to fling myself from that stone ledge. The weight of shame pounded my body. It crushed the air out of my lungs. A viselike grip squeezed my temples. I was so nauseated that I dropped my head between my knees. I was supposed to be the umchin tdal. I had failed. I was not good enough to get into Harvard, where my parents desperately wanted me to go. And, it turned out, I was not good enough for Yale, where I thought I would belong.

I took a deep breath and opened the wood door. I stepped into the courtroom in a navy-blue dress with a delicate white feathery pattern, the only dress I owned that was nice enough to appear grown-up and professional. Three white men sat at a long conference table, all dressed in suits. One wore a tie. Seated already, at one of the opposing tables, was a blond-haired boy. He looked almost like a young man. He was almost as tall as his mother. Only in my memory did he remain seven years old.

I remember one of the men talking about the rules, phrases like "this arbitration is binding" and "you have given up the right to a trial by jury" and "both sides may call witnesses." I remember standing with my right hand raised and swearing to tell the truth. I remember little of my testimony.

"Why didn't you prescribe antibiotics?" the man in the navy-blue suit asked.

My lawyer protested. "I don't think that's pertinent to this case."

The man said, "The question regarding antibiotics is absolutely relevant. We note your objection, counselor, but the defendant will answer."

Unless a wound was an animal or a human bite—considered "dirty," in other words—pediatricians rarely gave prophylactic antibiotics, because a wound kept clean and dry was unlikely to get infected. If antibiotics were used for *every* cut or laceration a child ever suffered, antibiotic resistance would run rampant and superbacteria would reign.

I didn't say any of that. My lawyer had told me to keep my answers short. So I said, "There was no clinical indication for me to prescribe antibiotics."

I thought my answer was succinct but sufficient. In retrospect, I can see that all three white men in dark suits looked at me with skepticism.

One of my favorite ER attendings testified as an expert witness for the hospital. He was far more eloquent than I was about the appropriate use of antibiotics. After his testimony, he said to me, "The infection in his hand wasn't your fault. It was just unfortunate that a piece of glass was left in the same hand."

During a break in court, I went to the bathroom and stared at the mirror. My forehead glistened with oil. The skin under my right eye flickered as the muscle twitched underneath. I swallowed again and again to keep stomach acid from rising into my throat. As I walked back to the courtroom, I saw the attorney for the boy standing outside the door. I tried to pass him.

"Dr. Rho?" He introduced himself as if I didn't already know his name. I kept my eyes pinned to the lapel of his gray suit. He was a man in his thirties, medium build, medium height.

"You know, this is nothing personal. This is just business," he said.

I said nothing. I left him standing in the hallway.

Several months after I found out I was being sued, I sat in Louise's plushily carpeted office again. I held my breath.

Her ice-blue eyes were unwavering. "They found in favor of the plaintiff."

My breath rushed out. My shoulders slumped.

"It was for a ridiculously low amount. Three thousand dollars. A nuisance lawsuit."

"They chose to find for the plaintiff?" I was slow to grasp what had happened.

"They assigned your portion of damages to only fifteen hundred dollars."

I closed my eyes. I put my hands over my face. "I'm going to have to disclose that I lost a malpractice suit for the rest of my life. Certainly every time I apply for privileges at a hospital."

"They felt sorry for the lawyer. For all his time on a bad case. They threw him a bone."

"That's wrong." I was adamant about my idea of justice.

Louise arched her eyebrows at me. "Listen, a kid got an infection in his hand. Under the circumstances, the arbitration panel was reasonable with you."

"I don't see it that way."

Louise rolled her eyes. "You need to move on. You have the rest of your career in front of you."

"What a career," I said quietly.

∽

"You know she's going to sue," Rachel said.

Rachel and I were sitting in the atrium, having lunch. It had been six months since the lawsuit. We were both third-year residents, near the end of our training. We were talking about a case from the previous night, a toddler admitted for meningitis to the general pediatric service, on which I was the supervising third-year resident. I had come in that morning and examined the boy. He had been holding his neck in an awkward, contorted position because of severe throat swelling from tonsillitis. Not from meningitis. The boy was now in the OR for emergency surgery because his airway was about to close off.

"That mother is going to sue," Rachel said.

"I don't think so," I said.

"Are you kidding? The chance for her to make a lot of money? In this neighborhood?" Rachel was derisive about my seemingly naive attitude toward the poor and working-class population surrounding Children's Hospital.

I avoided looking at her. "The mother wasn't angry."

"She's going to go home and think about it. And choose money," Rachel said.

When I had told the boy's mother, a Latina immigrant, what was wrong with her son, she reached out and touched my hand. *"Gracias, gracias,"* she said.

"I was sued." The words came out of my mouth almost of their own volition.

"I know," Rachel said.

"How?" I said, my voice high-pitched.

"I heard what happened in Dr. Chan's clinic."

"Does everyone know?"

She looked down and hesitated before shaking her head.

"Great. Everybody knows." I pushed back in my chair, crossed my arms.

Rachel looked at me. "I was the first-year who admitted the kid to the peds service when he came back to the ER."

I looked back at her. "I read the chart. You knew the mother was angry. Why didn't you tell me?"

"I didn't think she was really going to sue," Rachel said.

My head dropped. "I can't believe I got sued."

"His hand got infected," she said.

I jerked my head up. "What do you mean?"

Rachel shrugged. "You left a piece of glass in his hand. It got infected. Come on, the kid had to be admitted to the hospital."

"His hand got infected because his mother ignored my wound-care instructions." I recrossed my arms, gripping my elbows, holding my body rigid.

"Are you sure you were clear about wound care?"

I said nothing, a deer caught in headlights. As one of the very few nonwhite residents in my program, I gave my fellow residents the benefit of the doubt. I had lied to the Latina mother that the second-year resident who had seen her son in the ER was not to blame for a misdiagnosis. The resident had most likely not examined the boy's throat; otherwise she would have seen the giant abscess on his tonsil, pus threatening to explode and obscure his airway and cause aspiration pneumonia. There had been clear negligence, and yet I covered for this white resident. The white residents in my program, however, were quick to judge me as inadequate, incompetent.

Almost everyone—Louise, the lawyer for the boy and his mother, the arbitrators, as well as the other residents, including Rachel—had assumed that the site of infection in the boy's hand was also where I left a piece of glass. That was not true. The infection was in a different place; it was where I had stitched a deep cut. I know I followed sterile protocol. I know I was clear about wound care.

The boy's mother failed to comply with my instructions. Maybe she ignored them because she still thought I was a nurse, not a doctor. Maybe she thought I was an unreliable authority figure because I was Asian and a woman. Perhaps she wasn't listening because she was distraught about her child's pain. Perhaps she couldn't hear because her ears were ringing from his relentless screaming.

But it is possible that I did not clean the cut thoroughly enough. It is possible that residual material and bacteria from a dirty playground remained in the wound and resulted in a child's admission to the hospital.

It is possible that I was sure I had done everything right, just like I had been sure I was worthy of getting into Yale.

The truth is, I will never know for certain what caused the infection of that boy's hand.

And a shard of glass remains embedded in my soul.

Chapter 7
A Mother's Burden

I woke up weeping. The bedroom was bright—baby-blue walls awash in early morning light. Broken sounds poured out of my mouth, echoing into still air. A deluge of tears washed down my cheeks, dripping onto my protruding belly. I was caught in the same looping nightmare: *On a clear sunny day, I sit with other mothers on a wooden bench in a playground. Children run, climb, shout gleefully. My son sits on the ground, rocking rhythmically. The other children point at him; the other mothers move away from me. I walk over to my son and enclose him in my arms. He continues rocking, oblivious to my touch.*

This was the recurring dream that haunted me while I was pregnant with my second child. A boy. His sex was detected by amniocentesis, because at my age the risk of birth defects was too high to be ignored. I didn't know why I kept having the same dream. Maybe I was manifesting what was my worst nightmare at the time: having an autistic son. I knew I would love him no matter what, but as in my dream, I was terrified of how others would treat him, and I worried about whether I would have the patience and resilience to care for him, and whether his needs would be met if I wasn't there to help.

As a pediatrician, I knew too much. I knew all the things that could go wrong—the birth traumas, the chromosomal abnormalities, the brain damage. The dangers of being born. When I was pregnant with my daughter, I had nightmares that she was anencephalic, the result of a congenital defect resulting in a child without a brain. With my son, it was repetitive visions of him in a playground, rocking without end. I couldn't even see his face clearly, but I knew what he was doing—it was what I had witnessed many children with autism doing.

❩

It had been a beautiful day in September 2001. I was standing in the playground of my daughter's elementary school.

"Mommy, Mommy, this is Francesca!" Erin came running up to me, breathless and excited, with one of her kindergarten classmates.

I looked down at a pretty girl with blond hair and blue eyes. "Hi, Francesca, so nice to meet you."

She looked at me and smiled before running off.

"Francesca is getting her mommy!" Erin ran after her friend.

I waited, pushing and pulling fifteen-month-old Liam's red stroller back and forth, hoping he would continue napping. I peeked over the top. Liam always looked like an angel when he slept—soft, downy hair, cherubic cheeks, bowed lips captured in stillness.

"Hi, I'm Sienna, Francesca's mother." The petite, pretty woman raised her voice to be heard above the clamor of children shrieking, laughing, and crying all around us. A little boy stood next to Sienna, holding her hand.

"This is Leonardo. We call him Leo."

I smiled at the blond, blue-eyed boy. "Hi, Leo, so nice to meet you." He did not look at me. He did not smile back. He said nothing.

"The girls are asking for a playdate," Sienna said. "We'd love to have Erin come over tomorrow after school."

"Are you sure you don't mind?" I said.

"I'll call you so you know that Erin is safe with us," Sienna assured me.

In the late afternoon the next day, I put Liam in his stroller and walked to Sienna's house.

She answered the door holding Leo's hand. "The girls are in the family room. I told them they could have a few more minutes. Would you like something to drink?"

I entered the unassuming split-level house, carrying Liam in my arms. I followed Sienna to the kitchen, watching two-year-old Leo, knowing something was off. He held his small frame upright. It was strange that there was no jubilation in his steps, no impatient tugging on his mother's arm. He just obediently held on to her hand. I'd worked with autistic children during my residency and also as an attending—I had diagnosed a few children with autism, and the developmental specialist had confirmed their heartbreaking diagnoses.

"Sorry about the mess. We're starting a renovation," Sienna explained, referring to the cardboard boxes stacked in the narrow kitchen.

"No need to apologize. My house still looks like this, and we moved in two months ago."

"Where'd you come from?"

"Baltimore."

"What were you doing there?"

"My husband was doing a fellowship at Johns Hopkins, and I was teaching there. I'm a pediatrician."

"You're both doctors?"

"Unfortunately."

Sienna laughed. "My husband and I are both attorneys, but I left the law when Francesca was born."

"You're the third lawyer I've met since moving here who has decided to stay home with her kids. What does that say about the law?" I smiled.

Sienna laughed again. "I guess you made a better choice with medicine."

I shook my head. "I'm not sure about that." I made my answer sound ambivalent, not definite, because I didn't want to say out loud that I didn't like medicine. I wasn't ready to admit that I hated being a doctor.

"Are you going to practice here? You'd have a lot of patients just from Erin's class."

I shook my head again. "I'm taking what I'm calling a sabbatical." A sabbatical seemed like a palatable thing to say, an acceptable alternative to "I want to permanently leave medicine."

I had intended to tell Sienna the short version, not the messy details. Instead I told her that I went back to work when Erin was six weeks old, and I felt like I missed her childhood. That I missed her first step. That I was lucky to be around when she said her first word, "Elmo," but I was working when she first said "Mama." That her nanny told me about her childhood milestones, and my daughter grew up with someone else mothering her. I told Sienna that I worked part-time after Liam was born. But there is really no such thing as a part-time doctor. Being on call so many nights, weekends, and holidays, I missed my son's first step. And his first word. He said "Mama" to someone else. I wanted to be a different kind of mother than my mother had been to me. A mother who engaged with her children, asked how their day at school was, what they did with their friends. A mother who saw her children as individuals, not a collective. A mother who nurtured her children's dreams, encouraging them to find their own passions rather than imposing her dream on them.

Sitting at Sienna's ornate wood dining table, I reached for my glass of water and took a sip. I had not meant to share so much.

Sienna looked at me with compassion. "I thought I was going back to work after Frankie was born. But I couldn't do it."

"It's really true that a child changes everything," I said.

Sienna looked at Leo sitting quietly on the floor, next to her chair. "After Frankie was born, we built our dream house with a backyard bordering a state park. It was gorgeous—the trees, the view, the quiet. The house had multiple decks and a beautiful in-ground pool. It took us two years to build. It had everything we wanted."

"It sounds like a bucolic paradise," I said.

"It was," she said.

"Why did you leave?"

"When Leo was two years old, he was still not talking. I thought, *He's a boy.* But there were signs. Loud noises upset him, or too many people, too many new faces. Leo doesn't get violent. He just shuts down. Our pediatrician sent us to a specialist. He said Leo was autistic."

I asked Sienna if Leo was getting the multitude of interventions that could help children with autism—cognitive therapy, occupational therapy, physical therapy, speech therapy, behavioral therapy. I knew the earlier the intervention, the better the outcome.

Sienna smiled grimly. "We sold our dream home and moved to this town because of the quality of services they supposedly give to autistic children. We kept asking. Those bureaucrats kept dragging their feet. But one of the benefits of being an attorney is that people take you seriously when you threaten to litigate."

"How are you managing?" I asked. "Does your husband help?"

"My mother helps when she can. My husband works in the city— gone early in the morning and back late at night. You know what that's like."

It was the year 2001, and yet Sienna and I talked about her husband "helping." Not parenting. It was the twenty-first century. But Sienna and I might as well have been back in the 1950s, with fathers "working" and mothers raising children. I accepted without question that Sienna, not her husband, would be spending hours and hours with Leo in different therapies, and then devoting hours and hours more reinforcing all of it with him. Because I accepted the fact that mothers lived for their children, their families. Not for themselves.

"What about babysitters?" I asked.

Sienna shook her head. "Leo can barely tolerate my mother. It would be a disaster with a total stranger."

"But, Sienna, you can't keep doing all this by yourself."

"My life is about Leo. And Frankie, of course. What would I do, anyway?" she said dismissively.

"Go to a bookstore and drink coffee and read romance novels. Or take up knitting. Learn yoga."

Sienna smiled. "That sounds great, but it's not realistic. Leo needs me."

"But you'll burn out and lose your mind," I said. "I'll be happy to babysit Leo."

"That's really kind of you," she said. "I'll think about it."

She never took me up on my offer to babysit Leo.

❧

After months of unshared childcare for a fifteen-month-old and a five-year-old in this suffocating suburb, I asked my husband if we could hire a babysitter for a few hours a week, so I could get some reprieve. (He left before our children woke up and got home hours after they went to sleep.)

"My mother would be happy to come on Wednesdays," he said.

"Really?" My voice rose in pitch, hopeful and tremulous.

"She missed Erin and Liam so much when we lived in Philly and Baltimore. I'm sure she'll be happy to babysit," he said.

"But she always has plans for her days off," I said, still skeptical.

"She only works part-time. She can do those things on Fridays. I'll talk to her," he said.

She came the first Wednesday and absorbed my gratitude with a complacent smile. The next Wednesday, she stayed three hours instead of four. The Wednesday after that, she said she was having dinner with friends and had to leave early. She stayed less than three hours.

Then my husband said that the dentist his mom worked for had offered her more hours, and she was torn between the extra money and how much she wanted to see her grandchildren. I suggested we pay her. He said she didn't want the money exchanged in the open. So we established a pattern: at the end of another short Wednesday afternoon with her grandchildren, she would start hugging and kissing them goodbye. That was my cue. I would run up to my bedroom, grab my wallet, and rush to the mudroom before her. With a hundred dollars in my hand, I would grope inside her purse for a spot between her wallet and keys so she could easily find the money.

She would appear in the doorway, her eyebrows raised.

I would nod to her purse on the bench. "Thanks for coming," I would say, my lips stretched into a smile.

"Oh, of course! You're welcome. I'll see you next Wednesday," she would say.

A few months into this intolerable arrangement, I spoke to my husband about stopping it.

"Charlene can now come on Mondays and Wednesdays," I said, referring to our normal babysitter.

"But my mom enjoys seeing Erin and Liam," he said.

"We can pay Charlene for both days with what we pay your mother."

"But my mom needs the money."

"Your mother owns two houses, neither of which have mortgages."

"How can you suggest that she stop seeing her grandchildren?"

The payments to his mother dragged on for almost two years, until we moved to Pittsburgh.

His mother liked to say she had been at the forefront of feminism. She was proud of the fact that she had burned her bra in the '70s, along with a few women in her neighborhood—all suburban stay-at-home mothers. It was a single, drunken gesture of rebellion against their husbands, but she would embellish the story, going on and on about a small bonfire in a backyard one summer night. Never mind that the next morning she was wearing another bra, supporting the status quo. According to her, her husband couldn't cook, could barely boil water, and never did housework, but her son had once vacuumed the living room while she was at work. She said that she had "raised a wife" for me. She expected gratitude, so I thanked her.

My father-in-law never complained about the three jobs he juggled for years to support his family. He only spoke about it with humor—the early mornings he spent with a friend delivering newspapers, or the late nights he hauled phone books to his neighbors, in addition to his day job working retail in a drugstore. He would joke about how fast he had to drive his car through the dark, on curving roads, to finish deliveries before sunrise. With no high school diploma himself, he wanted better for his two children. So he worked harder, took out loans, and afforded them college educations at Notre Dame and Villanova. He expected no gratitude, just their happiness. When I married my husband, I thought he was like his father—generous, loving, self-sacrificing. I could not have been more wrong. He was like his mother.

Sienna and I sat at a picnic table in her backyard, the late-afternoon sun floating on a blue horizon. Erin and Francesca played with Barbie Princesses, pretending the dolls could fly, soaring through spring sky, the girls running to keep up. Leo walked along the perimeter of the fence, slowly and deliberately. Liam sat at my feet, banging plastic toys together. Occasionally he looked up at me, his face breaking into a wide smile, joyful inarticulations coming from his throat.

"Look at Liam! He is such a happy baby," Sienna said.

"I'm lucky he's a happy baby. Otherwise I couldn't survive all those Mommy and Me classes. Mommy and Me Cooking. Mommy and Me Music. Mommy and Me Art. They're driving me up a wall," I said. "I'm so bored that I want to cry." Immediately I felt remorse.

What kind of mother complains about spending time with her child?

I had decided to take this time away from medicine to raise my children and watch them grow up. I'd expected to be happy, devoting my days to my children's needs. Instead I was miserable. At first I blamed the other stay-at-home mothers. Rather than talking about books or art or geopolitical events of consequence, they obsessed about the sleeping habits of their infants and toddlers, their own lack of sleep, their never-ending weight gain, and their lack of time and energy to work out. It was all so maddening. I didn't want to admit it, but I hated those Mommy and Me classes. I plastered a smile on my face, but my eyes strayed to the clock. I would count down the minutes until music or art or cooking class was over. Even as Liam smiled and swayed, tapping a tambourine; even as he swirled blue and green paint into indistinguishable blobs; even as he laughed while making pancakes and licked his plump fingers covered with egg yolk and flour. The fierce beauty of those moments could not mitigate the mind-numbing, slow-motion nature of time spent with a toddler.

Sienna made no comment. She didn't say that she and Leo didn't take any Mommy and Me classes, that they never would.

I felt like an idiot.

"Are you going back to work?" she asked.

"Yes," I said. "As a doctor in training, I did thirty-six-plus hours of work nonstop without sleep, and sometimes without eating. But I swear, the day-to-day work of raising small children is harder."

Sienna laughed.

The cycle of laundry, dishes, and cleaning up toys and fallen food from the floor seemed endless. Always catering to the constant demands of young children. Starting the day with cries of "Mommy, Mommy!" and ending the day the same way. I was unhappy being a doctor, and now I was unhappy being a stay-at-home mother. I didn't know where I belonged.

"I took care of poor kids in the inner city—the kids were great. But everything else was an enormous pain in the ass," I said.

It seemed inevitable that I would return to the practice of medicine. Medical school trains you to be a doctor and not much else. When my mother-in-law would watch my children for a couple of hours, I usually went to the town library. Libraries are soothing to me. Surrounded by shelves and shelves of books, I can breathe easier, think more clearly. I had bought some old-fashioned black-and-white composition notebooks, looking forward to the novels I would write, although I told no one what I wanted to do. Nothing happened. And I came to the conclusion that I was qualified only to be a doctor. I knew how to be a doctor. I thought I should go back to what I knew.

"Suburban kids need good doctors too," Sienna said.

"True. But they don't need me," I said. "Do you miss the law?"

"No, I was never passionate about it. My husband loves it."

"Don't you wish he was passionate about laundry?" I said.

Sienna laughed. "Or the dishes."

I laughed along. "Just some help cleaning up the toys strewn everywhere would make me really happy."

"My husband is great with toy management. Frankie's collection of dolls and their paraphernalia alone can take hours to sort."

"I'm glad he's helpful."

"I shouldn't complain. And Frankie's already a responsible kid. She's so protective of Leo." Sienna paused. "What does a six-year-old really know?"

"Kids sense things." I believed that Frankie instinctually knew that Leo could be vulnerable.

Sienna looked pensive. "I wish she didn't. We've established a trust for Leo, and we've named my mother as trustee. But someday Francesca will be responsible for her brother."

I looked at Frankie playing with Barbies. She and Erin were intent on dressing and undressing their dolls with different combinations of outfits—ball gowns, miniskirts, bikinis. Frankie paired a Barbie in a pink tutu and a glittery tiara with a Ken doll in a Hawaiian shirt and board shorts. The two of them drove off in a pink camper, Barbie smiling vacantly into the sunset.

Chapter 8
New Year's Day

Staring at the peeling floral wallpaper in our dimly lit kitchen, I feel the first regret of the New Year. It is noon, January 1, 2003. I am hosting a Korean New Year's banquet, and my sisters and their families will be here in an hour. I wonder why I chose to do *this*: this meal, this year.

I walk across the white-and-navy ceramic tile floor, chipped in so many places that I yet again lament the fact that I haven't replaced it. I swing open a creaky cabinet door and extract the largest pot I own. As I fill it with water, I stare with dismay at the stained enamel sink, no longer pristine white. I switch on the bulb above the grimy, formerly white range stuck in an awkward corner of the kitchen. The light flickers. I hold my breath. The weak, yellowing halo stays on.

Although we have spoken for many years about gathering for a traditional Korean New Year's celebration, this year will be the first. If we had a brother, the jangsohn, we would be going to his house because it would fall to his wife to cook and host the meal. Instead my sisters and I remain in the shadow of the missing son. We all live in the metropolitan New York area. But in two months I will follow my husband to Pittsburgh for his career, and I will be returning to the practice of pediatrics, no longer a stay-at-home mom.

Still, I regret the invitation I impulsively extended to my sisters when I saw them over the Christmas holidays. Christmas matters because of our acquired families, our children. But for my sisters and me, it is Seollal, or New Year's Day, that has resonance. When we lived in Korea, we celebrated Seollal on the first day of the lunar calendar, like millions of Koreans on the peninsula. But now, like other Koreans in the diaspora, away from our homeland, we celebrate Seollal on the first day of the solar calendar.

I have already made pots of steamed white rice and mounds of *jhap chae*—clear vermicelli noodles sautéed with beef, mushrooms, onions, carrots, and spinach—and assorted small side dishes called *banchan*. I have also cheated and catered *gimbap*, cooked rice seaweed rolls, and *mandu twigim*, fried pork dumplings. But I haven't started on the *tteok guk*. Rice cake soup.

Tteok guk is the soul of Seollal. And there is an art to cooking tteok guk, a deceptively simple dish. To get it right, one has to be vigilant and patient. *Tteok*, or rice cake, the heart of the soup, is capricious. Cook the sliced white ovals too long and they turn to mush; cook them too briefly and they retain the consistency of rocks. The list of ingredients is spare: beef broth, rice cake, eggs, scallion, sesame seeds. But it's the proportion of each component in relationship to the others that's important. And the order in which the five elements are combined is crucial to the taste.

Start with the broth, and then slide in slivers of rice cake. Eggs, whisked with a little salt, have to be stirred in before the scallions, or else the eggs clump around the minced green onions, creating chunks, not wisps. Crushed sesame seeds go in last; otherwise the soup tastes burnt. Sometimes *mandu*, or meat dumplings, can be added. But that changes the soup, and then it's called *tteok mandu guk*—rice cake and dumpling soup. My sister Sophia prefers tteok mandu guk. But not me. I am a purist at heart. Any other time of year I will eat tteok mandu guk gladly, but not on New Year's Day. Because Seollal is always about tteok guk.

When my sisters and I were growing up, whether it was in Kampala or Petersburg or New Jersey, my mother made rice cake soup every New Year's Day. She used to say, *"You can't grow another year older and wiser if you don't eat tteok guk on Seollal."* New Year's Day, not New Year's Eve, is the time of celebration for Koreans. It is our Thanksgiving. We reunite with family members and feast on an elaborate meal prepared by the host family. There is no such thing as a potluck dinner for Koreans. Guests are not expected to bring anything, other than the honor of their presence. After every grandmother, uncle, older sister, and youngest cousin has gorged themselves on the plethora of flavorful dishes, the children perform a time-honored tradition, *sebae*, in front of each adult. Boys bow; girls curtsy. And they must recite a specific phrase: *"In the New Year, may you receive much good fortune."* In exchange for these symbolic gestures of goodwill, the children are rewarded with cash. When we were young, my sisters and I competed to see who could win the most money.

In my kitchen, the maple cutting board clatters on the warped and slanted counter as I slice beef into slender two-inch strips to make broth. Blood oozes along the wood grain and drips onto the blue-speckled Formica. I think, *I should have bought three pounds of beef instead of two.*

My sisters are petite women; none of them top five feet. In pictures of the four of us, at five feet two inches, I am the bump that breaks the straight line. But their husbands are all tall, and my oldest sister's husband is a big man. Susan tries to keep up with her husband in the amount of food consumed. At age three, their only son can eat at a pace that will no doubt match his father's very soon. Rather than being disturbed by this potential problem, Susan is proud of her son. As a pediatrician, I feel duty bound to warn her against what I believe is permissive parenting. But despite my supposed expertise in childrearing, Susan dismisses me. She tells me that unconditional love is good for a child. She says she wishes she'd gotten even a drop of it from our mother. Susan is a former clinical psychologist who now devotes her life to her son and has not worked outside the home since his birth.

I sigh and press my lips into a thin line as the stainless-steel pot squeaks on the uneven surface of the old cooking range. Dense constellations of bubbles erupt on the water's surface. Steam rises and soon obscures the faded blue flowers on the worn wallpaper, which is coming undone at the seams.

My sister Sophia, older than me by two years, has no patience for Susan's parenting. She tells her seven-year-old daughter and four-year-old son that she runs a boot camp. Sophia is all about scheduling. She is so organized and determined that she involves both her children in a frenzy of activity, six days a week. They race from school to the ice-skating rink, to piano lessons, to soccer games. I tell her to slow down or she will run herself and her children ragged. But she quotes from the Bible instead: "Idle hands are the devil's workshop." Sophia has rheumatoid arthritis but works full-time as a pharmacist, volunteers in her children's classrooms, and flatly refuses to stop the frenetic pace of her life.

I drop shreds of beef into scalding water and add *dashida* seasoning. I swirl the stew meat around. Clear water clouds into broth. I worry: *Will there be enough?*

My younger sister, Clara, doesn't understand any of our arguments. She and her fiancé live in Manhattan, work miserable hours as attorneys, and get takeout most nights, unless they actually go out to a restaurant. Clara is childless and not about to change that anytime soon. I tell her that thirty-three is not so young, but she rolls her eyes and tells me that she has plenty of time to have children. Someday. She disdains as out of touch the advice of a sister older than her by five years: "Why should I have children?" Probably a legacy of being raised by our mother.

Paralyzed by anger and guilt, my sisters and I avoid the subject of our mother. We cannot all agree on how to deal with her willful isolation and increasingly erratic behavior, and it's easier not to argue. But we are united in our failure. We all married non-Korean men, a moral crime in my mother's eyes. Even Susan's husband, the Chinese man among the white brothers-in-law, is not good enough. Two of the brothers-in-law are physicians and the one yet to be is a lawyer, professions my mother considers successful. But that is still not good enough.

My mother remained so opposed to this notion of tainting thousands of years of pure Korean blood that she did not attend Susan's wedding, the first among the four sisters. Although she was present at my nuptials, she came only grudgingly. I remember pleading with her as her face remained unmoved, as smooth as alabaster. *"How could you do this to me?"* she said, her voice cold and hard. It was the first time in my life I had disobeyed my mother's wishes. She did not attend the rehearsal dinner the night before my wedding, and until I saw her seated in the front pew of the poorly lit St. Catherine of Bologna Catholic Church, I did not know she would come.

Susan bitterly points out that our mother is too much of a snob to have missed my wedding—who would take the credit for me becoming a doctor and then crowning my achievement by marrying another doctor? Certainly not my father, another failure in my mother's eyes, and not just because they are divorced. To say that divorce is rare in Korea is an understatement. Koreans do not get divorced, especially those in the upper class, like my parents. My mother still hasn't told her family fourteen years after her divorce, and she probably never will, because of her overwhelming sense of shame, a character trait I inherited. She rarely visits Korea, and her mother and sister last visited her when I was a child. She no longer speaks to her family on the telephone. The last time she got a phone call, it was news that her father had died. So she writes letters, blue folded notes with "aerogram" printed on them. I imagine she can create a parallel universe on those thin azure sheets, one in which she is happy, one in which her family does not have to worry about her.

In the tight confines of my dreary kitchen, the fragrance of cooking meat fills the air. My knife blade falls across the bodies of the scallions, releasing a bitter yet refreshing scent. I finish the rest of my mise en place: prying apart oval slices of rice cake, resisting the starch sticking them together like glue; cracking open large brown eggs into a white bowl and whisking them with a little salt; grinding sesame seeds in the ceramic mortar and pestle. The nutty, nostalgic aroma of crushed seeds bathes my nostrils, reminding me of all the meals my mother cooked during my childhood.

Until my children were born, I did not know how to make tteok guk. When I was growing up, my mother would shoo me away from the kitchen whenever I asked to help. She would say, *"You need to study. You are going to do important things when you are a doctor. Cooking is easy. I can teach you that later."* Except later never came. To learn how to cook Korean food, I bought a cookbook written in English by a Korean American who interspersed her mother's recipes with personal family stories—about her grandmother, a renowned chef in what is now North Korea, and her mother, the primary breadwinner, struggling to start a restaurant in New York's East Village. Estranged from my mother, I can't call her to ask if she uses more soy sauce and less sugar in her bulgogi than the author suggests, if she adds more scallions and less sesame seeds to her tteok guk. I have to rely on my memories of tasting her soup. With the guide of a cookbook, I am trying to re-create my mother's tteok guk.

Like a cyclone of motion, my six-year-old daughter bursts into the cramped kitchen. "Mommy, Mommy, you have to help me!" She careens around, making miniature circles on the ceramic tile floor.

"Erin, please, stop the noise."

She fights to contain her energy, but her arms flail with each word. "I need your help putting on my Korean princess costume!"

"Do you have to wear that today?" I am referring to the *hanbok*, or traditional dress, worn by women in Korea for special occasions. I had bought Erin a miniature pink-and-white one fashioned like that of a Joseon-dynasty princess, as a Halloween costume.

"Yes, yes, yes!" Her eyes are wide, her head nodding vigorously. "I'll get more money if I'm dressed Korean!"

I try to reason with her. "I don't think your cousins are coming dressed in hanboks. Can't you just put on your regular clothes?"

"No!" She is impatient with my lack of understanding. "Mommy, please, let me wear it!"

I'm defeated. "Okay, okay. Just bring it down. I'll help you."

She thunders upstairs, her shout of thanks echoing in the stairwell.

I remember dressing up in my mother's hanboks as a child on New Year's Day, to do my sebae with my sisters. I remember us laughing. I can't blame my daughter for wanting to do the same.

⁓

"Why didn't you start the tteok guk sooner?" Sophia asks the moment she steps into my kitchen.

My sisters have arrived in a flurry of noise and activity, one after another. Their children play with mine downstairs in the family room while they set two tables—putting out the fine bone china, glasses, and silver chopsticks for the adults' table and the paper bowls, plastic cups, and wooden chopsticks for the children's table. I hear snatches of my sisters' chatter and laughter. One of them scolds a child not to run in the living room. One of them tells me that the fried pork dumplings are delicious, while another sister wanders into the kitchen, chewing on seaweed-covered gimbap filled with rice, beef, spinach, daikon, egg, and carrots.

I dip my Korean spoon into simmering soup and take a cautious taste. The beef broth has infused heartiness into the rice cake ovals; the scallions are bright and tangy; the eggs are light and delicate; the crushed sesame seeds have been absorbed into nuttiness. And the slices of rice cake are soft, but structured. All five ingredients have melded, and harmony has emerged. I ladle the soup into round celadon bowls. We sit down to eat.

"Next year we should have it in my house. My kitchen is bigger. And it will be renovated," Sophia says.

I nod.

"Why didn't you put mandu in the tteok guk? You know, it would taste better that way," she asserts, wanting her dumplings.

"Because I didn't want to," I snap. Immediately, I regret my curtness. The new year will not bode well if we start with a fight. "Tteok guk is what we always have on New Year's Day," I amend, passing out *gim*—roasted and salted seaweed squares—to crumble into the soup.

"It's boring. It would taste better with mandu," Sophia insists.

"Tteok guk is comfort food." I bite on a sliver of rice cake, savoring the firm yet yielding center and the play of flavors and textures—so simple, yet so complex.

Sophia shrugs. "Whatever."

She will never understand my love of tteok guk.

Immediately after the meal, our children clamor to do their sebae. We decide that each adult couple will take turns sitting on the sofa while all the children bow and curtsy together. That way the children will prostrate themselves four times instead of eight. Sophia and Clara give one dollar to each child. I do the same. But not Susan. She distributes twenty-dollar bills in shiny red envelopes. The children shriek with delight at their windfall. When the adults look at her askance, she says that it will be Chinese New Year in a matter of weeks, and we should celebrate that too.

Clara, characteristically quiet through most of the chaos, approaches me with her coat draped over her arm. She intends to go into the office, billing even more hours on this holiday.

"Why don't you stay for coffee?" I say, hoping to extend her visit.

She brushes me off, as expected. "I can't. I'm going to trial next week."

I am resigned. "It's good to see you. Let's get together for dinner in the city before I move."

She shakes her head. "I don't know how long the trial will be."

We still have time. You can't squeeze me in? Instead I just nod.

But Clara hesitates in her haste to leave my house. She slowly pulls on her coat, adjusts her scarf, carefully inserts each finger into her gloves. I wait.

"I got a letter from Mom," she says, her words rushed.

I close my eyes and hold my breath. When I open my eyes, I see Clara staring at the broken tiles in my kitchen floor.

"What does she want?" I ask.

"She needs money."

"What else is new?" I say.

"She's getting worse. She used to ask for a couple of hundred dollars every few months, and I would just send a check. But this time, she wrote me some story about an emerald that is worth thirty thousand dollars. But she will sell it to me for twenty thousand."

Clara speaks softly to try to hide the fact that she is crying, but her tears fall faster. I try to put my arm around her shoulders, but she rebuffs me. I understand. Sometimes, one touch and I come unraveled.

"It's not your fault," I say. "You know she tried that with me. When I told her I couldn't buy the emerald, she stopped speaking to me. She moved on to Sophia, then Susan, and now you."

"What do I write back? I know she needs money, but twenty thousand dollars! If she needs that kind of money, she needs to sell her house." Clara is literally wringing her hands.

"The roof is falling in. But she clings to that house, insisting it will be worth a million dollars in a few years. How do you reason with a delusional woman?" I say, rehashing old ground.

"If only we could get her out of that house!" Clara twists her scarf into a knot.

"We tried. We can't," I say softly.

Silence and failure hang between us.

Clara wipes away her tears, her mask back in place. "I have to go. I'll call you about dinner." She slips on her shoes and steps out the door.

I lean the weight of my body against the worn kitchen wallpaper, rest my head on the wall. I want to close my eyes and go to sleep. Instead I take a deep breath. I go back to the party.

My children and their cousins are running around my living room, shouting with joy, dropping crumbs carelessly. I do not curb their enthusiasm.

"I guess they're having a good time. But they're making too much noise," Sophia says, trying to rein in her children, with no success.

"Leave them alone. You're too uptight," Susan says.

"No, Sue, just because your kid is out of control doesn't mean my kids should be too. My children know what is expected of them," Sophia says as she pointedly stares at Susan.

I interrupt before things escalate. "Okay, you guys, no fighting."

Susan and Sophia live in the same development of cookie-cutter houses, only blocks apart. They rely on each other: picking up each other's kids from school, carpooling to activities, and trading babysitting. Most of the time it works. But they clash in their methods of discipline, and their children play together often. I frequently get complaints from one about the other, especially in the aftermath of a battle. Like our mother, neither has made close friends. Maybe because they have each other and feel they don't need anyone else.

"Do you remember the last New Year's we spent in Korea?" Susan suddenly asks, her voice wistful. "It was the last time we saw our cousins."

Her yearning is too much to bear. I look away.

On Seollal 1972, my parents, sisters, and I lived in Seoul. We took a taxi to a relative's house in the suburbs. I can't remember which one. I think it must have been someone on my mother's side of the family, but I could be mistaken since my father's family is from Seoul and my mother's family is from Gwangju. By the time we arrived, groups of people occupied every room. My sisters and I went to play with the other children, plotting ways to get more money from the adults when the time came for the bows and curtsies. We were allowed to eat everywhere and run while doing it, something quite unusual in our everyday lives. I remember a whirlwind of sound—adults laughing, children yelling, music playing. I remember my mother happy. At the end of the night, I was the child who made the most money. I paid for our taxi ride home. I was proud of my accomplishment. I couldn't stop smiling as I leaned against my sisters, excitedly comparing our earnings, looking out at the lights illuminating Seoul. I thought, *What a wonderful end to the first day of the new year.* I didn't know we would be moving to Uganda in just a few months.

After my sisters go home, I am left with the remnants of tteok guk. The broth has congealed from the starch of rice cake ovals, which are now bloated and misshapen. Beef strips, shriveled and discolored, stick out of the soup like brown twigs. Dried yellow egg tendrils cling to the sides of the stainless-steel pot. I pick up the dirty dishes from the dining room table and take them into my woeful kitchen. The peeling wallpaper, the mismatched melamine cabinets, the stained sink are thrown into sharp relief by the dismal lighting. We were supposed to be renovating the kitchen this year, not moving to Pittsburgh. But my husband has decided that he's unhappy with his job. My life and my children's lives revolve around his needs, his wants. Like my father, he dictates where our family lives, what our family does.

I tell myself that I'm glad I got to see my sisters before I have to go through yet another disorienting shift in geography. But I have to stop myself from dropping to my knees on that broken-tile floor. I want to mourn the girls that my sisters and I used to be. I want to mourn the woman my mother was. But I do not cry. Instead, I wash the plates, the pots, the chopsticks.

I wonder if I could have changed what happened the following year. I wonder if I could have stopped my mother from trying to commit suicide.

Chapter 9
Leaving Medicine

He's sitting too quietly for a seven-year-old was my first thought when I entered the exam room. "Hi, Tommy, how are you doing?"

He blinked his clear-blue eyes at me and then swiveled his towhead to his father, a burly man with nondescript brown hair.

"It's nice to meet you, Mr. Hayes. What brings you to the clinic?" I said.

"Good to meet you, Doctor." He sounded almost shy. "Tommy's got a sore throat."

I sat down, and Mr. Hayes followed suit in a gray plastic chair next to the exam table.

"Does he have a fever? Runny nose? Cough?" I asked in rapid succession.

"I'm sorry, but I haven't been paying much attention with the funeral."

I looked up from my notes. "Funeral?"

"Tommy's mother passed last week." He looked down at his calloused hands. "She had Huntington's." He looked up again, his face impassive.

"I'm so sorry," I said, stunned.

He tilted his head toward his son. "I got the kids to worry about."

"How many children do you have?"

"Two teenagers and Tommy. He's my youngest."

"Have you thought about grief counseling for you and your children?"

He shook his head. "I'm in construction. I only get paid if I work. My sister's living with us for now."

"Are you sure? I can recommend some good counselors who take Medicaid," I said, looking at Tommy tapping his white sneakers against the metal exam table, his blond head bowed.

Tommy's father nodded but said nothing. I could tell by his stony face that the conversation was over as far as he was concerned.

I stopped asking questions and examined Tommy. His throat was bright red but had no exudates, which would be more indicative of a bacterial infection. Still, I suspected he had strep throat. Mr. Hayes didn't sound surprised when I called the next day with the positive result of the throat culture. Tommy needed antibiotics, which I offered to call in to a pharmacy near his home, but Mr. Hayes had already made an appointment to see me because his older son also had a sore throat. I told him to bring any and all members of the family with a sore throat—we would treat them all. After I hung up the phone, I sat and read through Tommy's entire chart. The more I read, the more my dread grew, and the greater my effort to keep breathing evenly.

What if you could take a blood test and find out for certain that you had a terrible disease? What if you knew that this disease would slowly rob you of your mind and memories, and it had already killed your mother and grandfather?

Huntington's disease is incurable, and an uncommon variant called juvenile Huntington's disease devastates children, with initial symptoms ranging from seizures to muscle rigidity to scholastic and social difficulties. The earlier the onset, the faster the progression. Children with JHD have such rapid deterioration that death inevitably occurs within ten years. Each child of an HD parent has a 50 percent chance of inheriting the HD gene.

Tommy had abnormal brain scans and a history of seizures. With Tommy's mother dying so young and so quickly from the disease, and the way HD gene mutations amplify with each successive generation, along with Tommy's medical history, the implications for him could be catastrophic.

∽

The tips of my fingers went numb as I waited on the cold steel table in the freezing room. The thin hospital gown served as yet another transmitter of cold and did nothing to dissipate the goose bumps all over my body. I wished my mind would go numb. But it raced back to the day of my accident and why I was shivering in this radiology suite, dreading the coming procedure.

"You're in shock. You should go to the hospital," the EMT had said. Instead I drove back home. By then, my neck and back had seized into immobility and the pain was excruciating.

I ended up in the ER. I had MRIs of my neck and back done quickly because as a doctor, not just a patient, I was afforded preference. Two discs in my lower back were herniated and the trapezius muscle attached to my neck and shoulders was torn, the forces of impact having been absorbed by my body instead of dissipating through the body of my car. I was told to follow up with an orthopedic surgeon. I chose to make an appointment with a physiatrist, a doctor who specializes in physical medicine and rehabilitation. My reasoning: a medical option was better than a surgical one. When the physiatrist examined me, I demonstrated weakness and decreased mobility of my right leg; I could not bend at the waist. When I walked, I dragged my right foot, my gait uneven. The physiatrist recommended a series of steroid injections into my vertebral column to alleviate pain and reduce swelling of the damaged nerves.

I thought I would be cured if I followed my doctor's recommendations. I could not wrap my head around the fact that I was now a patient with chronic back pain.

I limped into the exam room to find Mr. Hayes with a taller, larger version of Tommy. Neither of the boys looked like their father; I assumed they resembled their mother. Tommy's older brother complained he couldn't swallow. He said his girlfriend had a sore throat the week before. I teased him that he shouldn't be kissing girls with sore throats. He blushed. His father smiled a little. Empirically, I prescribed antibiotics for Tommy's brother but sent a swab of his throat for culture to confirm strep. I asked Mr. Hayes about his daughter.

"She's coming in tomorrow to see you, Doctor."

"That sounds like a plan, Mr. Hayes."

Tommy's sister was a brown-haired female version of him. Her throat wasn't red or inflamed, no sign of exudates.

"Your brothers both have strep throat, but it looks like you escaped. I'm still going to send a throat culture, just in case."

She nodded, avoiding my gaze.

"Well, this is an appointment for a full physical, so we need to talk about a few things—school and home, sex and drugs," I nudged, once her father was out of the exam room.

She shrugged, looking down at her worn-out sneakers. "I don't drink or take drugs. School's okay—boring but not bad."

"And how are things at home with your mother gone?"

She shrugged again. "It's weird."

"It's weird to lose your mother when you're still a child."

"I'm not a child. I cook for my father and brothers—there isn't anyone else to do it."

"That's got to be hard. Do you have any friends you can talk to?"

"Nobody's mother has died," she said flatly. "Except mine."

"I think talking to a therapist would help you," I said.

"Whatever," she said, her head bent, gnawing on her fingernails.

I persisted. "Can I make you an appointment with a grief counselor?"

"I don't want to talk about it." Her long brown hair was a curtain between us. She may have looked like her mother, but she acted like her father.

"Okay then, it's time to talk about sex," I said.

She pushed herself upright, rigidly locking her arms against the exam table.

"Are you having sex with boys or girls or both?" I asked.

She shook her head violently. "I'm not having sex!"

"Okay, okay. I'm just asking." We sat in silence for a moment. "I believe you," I said.

"There's a boy I like in history class," she said, her voice barely above a whisper. "But I don't think he knows I'm alive."

"I'm sure he notices you—you're so pretty." I smiled.

"Sometimes I catch him looking at me." A smile flitted across her face before it dissolved into distressed folds around her beautiful blue eyes. "I miss my mom! I wish I could tell her all these things, but she isn't here. Why isn't she here?" she sobbed.

I tried to put my arms around her, but she pushed away. "I'm sorry," I said, swallowing a sudden knot in my throat. I could not bear to imagine my children in her position, trying to stem an ocean wave of grief. I shut down my emotions, my usual operating procedure for dealing with patients in pain.

When Mr. Hayes came back into the exam room, I sent his daughter for routine yearly blood tests. I told him that her physical was normal and she should receive the appropriate immunizations for a fifteen-year-old.

"There's one more thing, Mr. Hayes."

"Yes, Doctor?"

"I noticed in Tommy's chart some tests that were done a long time ago. Do you know if Tommy had a scan of his brain recently? An MRI or a CT scan?"

"I don't know much about that, Doctor."

"That's okay, Mr. Hayes."

"I'm sorry, but Tommy's mother brought him to all the doctor visits."

"Do you remember the last time Tommy had a seizure?"

He shook his head again. "When he was three or four?"

"That's okay, Mr. Hayes. Thank you for being so patient with my questions."

He didn't ask why I was asking those questions.

⟋⟍

I shivered on the procedure table in the radiology suite, waiting for my second steroid injection. The first one, done a few weeks earlier, had been excruciating. And it made my limp worse. I could still feel the needle penetrating my skin, pushing deep past muscle and touching nerve—pain so shattering it obliterated everything else. I kept praying this injection wouldn't be so bad.

It was worse. I didn't think that was possible, but it was. I sat in my car after the procedure and wept. I did not want surgery, so I did physical therapy and investigated alternative medicine. I tried acupuncture—anything was better than surgery and possible paralysis.

At work I moved woodenly, unable to swing toddlers onto the exam table or hop with five-year-olds or test the strength of teenagers because I couldn't hold back their arms as they pushed against me. Was their muscle tone normal, or was I just too physically weak to assess them properly? By the end of my usual ten-hour days, the pain in my back radiated down my right leg. My foot alternated between unbearable throbbing and numbness. I hobbled home.

I couldn't pick up my son, who was three years old at the time. He would come running down the hallway toward the front door when he saw me through the glass, the click of keys in the lock alerting him to my presence. I couldn't bend down to give him a hug. I patted his head as he wrapped his arms around my leg, jumping and shouting, "Mommy, Mommy, Mommy!" And I had to deny his request for "Up!" as he held his arms high above his head. Instead I had to pull away and sit on the wood floor, while he looked forlorn, as if I had rejected him. "It's okay," I would say with a smile, gesturing for him to come sit with me. He would gingerly perch on my crossed legs before running off to look for his older sister, my tibias too bony for comfort. He probably missed me hoisting him as high as I could, his face grinning down at me as I kissed his cheeks with resounding glee. It shattered me when he stopped asking for "Up!" I thought I was a better mother than my mother. I hugged my children every day. I read them bedtime stories, I tucked sheets and blankets around them, kissed them goodnight. Now it was painful to be the kind of mother I wanted to be.

My new physiatrist, a sensible woman, advised that I should think about going out on disability. "Temporarily," she said. Until I got better. When was that going to be? She didn't know. I approached both the chief of the division of general pediatrics and the chairman of the department of pediatrics and asked to have my work hours cut back. Their response: Yes. But they wanted a 30 percent decrease in my already part-time salary, in exchange for a 15 percent decrease in hours. When I protested, the white male chairman of pediatrics was particularly nasty. "I gave you a job when I didn't have to," he sneered. He shouted at me that I should be grateful—apparently furious that I, an Asian woman, was not silent and obedient. What I earned wasn't enough to pay my childcare costs. I resigned from my position as an assistant professor of pediatrics at Children's Hospital on January 1, 2004.

I thought at the time that I would be returning to the practice of medicine. I hadn't willingly become a doctor, but now it was all I knew, how I identified myself. As a good Korean daughter, I had felt obligated to go to medical school to please my immigrant parents, to fulfill their American Dream. I had yet to articulate out loud my desire to become a writer, to pursue my dream. And I had become a patient with chronic back pain. I felt vulnerable. I didn't know what was coming: Would my pain be bearable today, or would it be worse? And what about tomorrow? Being a doctor, I thought I would have an advantage in managing a chronic condition—I would be better prepared, less afraid of pain. Instead I knew too much and yet not enough.

Sometimes the pain in my back was so piercing that the only thing I could do was lie on the floor, perfectly still, and wait for the medications to work. Desperate, I went to a behavioral psychologist to try biofeedback. He told me about a child with juvenile rheumatoid arthritis, whose pain from her inflamed and swollen joints was unbearable until she learned to visualize a glass of water getting colder with each passing second. This imagery helped her lower her body temperature and decrease her inflammation and suffering. He asked me what I found soothing. I told him staring at waves coming onto a beach instilled a serenity that allowed my shoulders to fall away from my ears, my lungs to expand, my spine to stretch taller. The rhythmic motion of wave after wave hitting the sand was mesmerizing. The relentless nature of tides reminded me of the steadfast yet undulating quality of life itself.

The psychologist told me that pain pathways wore grooves into our brains that were difficult to modify, especially if they were interwoven with psychological trauma. Surviving a car accident was, by definition, a traumatic event. And other life events could contribute to the strands of pain that carved those neural grooves in our brains. He asked me what was going on in my life. I told him that I had left my job, where I'd had to tell the father of a seven-year-old that his son most likely had a devastating neurological disease. I told him my mother had tried to take her own life. I told him my father-in-law, who had been more of a father to me than the man biologically responsible for my birth, had suddenly died.

He said that in order to untangle my physical pain from its psychological triggers, I had to establish new neural pathways and patterns. He told me to conjure up the image of water washing ashore whenever my back started to throb. To meditate on that visual for as long as I could—a minute, five minutes, thirty minutes. I tried. But I found myself holding my breath, unable to allow my mind to go quiet while waves of pain slammed into my body, searing and blinding. I wept whenever he brought up the subject of trauma and loss. I stopped going to see him. I see now that I could not unravel the threads of my sexual trauma as a child from the trauma that I'd witnessed in the children who were my patients. Instead, loss upon loss grew and grew, a giant ball I could no longer swallow.

On my last day of work as a physician, I lingered. I said my goodbyes to the residents I'd supervised and the staff of the pediatric clinic as they left to go home. Then, alone, I sat at my desk and picked up the phone. I could not put off this call any longer. I dialed Tommy's father.

"Hello, Doctor, it's nice of you to call," he said, warmth in his voice.

I told him I needed to speak with him about Tommy and the history of Huntington's in the family.

"What about it?" he asked.

I said the abnormal test results in Tommy's chart disturbed me. I said that, with Tommy's mother having Huntington's and the genetic amplification of the disease, I was worried about Tommy.

"Are you saying Tommy has Huntington's?"

I said I didn't know. The only way to tell was for Tommy to take a blood test. I wasn't sure I would recommend it because Tommy was so young. But it was an option for his father to consider, given the possibility that Tommy may have juvenile Huntington's.

"I lost my wife to that damn disease. I don't want my kids to get it. But what's the point of getting the test?" For the first time, I heard a note of frustration in his voice.

I said he was right that there was no cure. But there were medications that could mitigate the seizures and depression if Tommy did have Huntington's.

"What's the right thing to do?" he asked.

I said I was sorry. That I wouldn't know what to do if I were in his place. I was telling the truth. I could not even imagine my children having Huntington's, never mind what I would do in his position. I refused to think about what Tommy's mother would have felt if she'd known about the turmoil she had left behind.

"Thank you, Doctor." He sounded genuinely grateful.

I told him I would not be working at the pediatric clinic anymore. Another doctor would be taking care of Tommy and his siblings.

He said he was sorry to see me go. He wished me luck.

I hung up the phone and blinked away the wetness pooling in my eyes. I closed Tommy's chart and stared at it. *My soul cannot survive another patient like this ever again.* I wondered what would happen to Tommy and his family, but, in truth, I didn't want to know. If I allowed myself to dwell on thoughts of Tommy and his father, the breath in my lungs would become trapped. My shoulders would seize into concrete. Images of that beautiful boy twitching and drooling in a hospital bed, while his father watched in agony, would engulf me. If I imagined his sister and brother standing outside Tommy's hospital room, wondering if this would be their fate someday, I would come undone.

I had agonized over every horrifying and heartbreaking diagnosis as a physician, as though it were one of my children who was sick and I had to try as hard as I could to make them better. But it seemed that no matter how hard I tried, I couldn't change anything for most of my patients; I couldn't make a difference—the same way I kept going back to the physiatrist and the psychologist to treat the pain that ravaged my back, neck, shoulders, and leg without any results. Instead I became a doctor who obsessively worried, sometimes unable to sleep, tortured by why a child's hemoglobin was low; why a baby was failing to thrive; whether the lump in a teenager's thigh was cancerous. I felt like I was in constant pain.

In my office, I gathered the last of my belongings: pictures of my children, the farewell cards expressing well wishes from the residents and staff, my pink stethoscope, my prescription pad and pens—the odds and ends of a physician's everyday practice. I tidied the paper clips and put away the stapler in the desk drawer. I put on my coat. I picked up the cardboard box. Before going down the stairs, I looked around the blank white walls and shut off the lights. I sat in my car and stared out the windshield into darkness for a long while.

As I steered out of the parking lot and past the rusted metal fences, away from the squat, unremarkable building that housed the pediatric clinic, I felt my shoulders fall, my neck no longer bound and twisted. I closed my eyes and exhaled audibly. I drove away from burden.

Chapter 10
The Korean Woman

It is a Saturday in March 2004, but snow flurries swirl as my daughter and I step out of her ballet school. She asks to go to Sam Bok for lunch. Again. I am reluctant to go to the small Korean grocery store in the middle of the Strip, but I agree. It is one of the infrequent ways my daughter, who is half Korean because of me, eats Korean food. Since September, we have established a routine: after ballet, we go to Sam Bok for lunch then Klavon's for ice cream.

We drive to the center of Pittsburgh's Strip District. Even with snow and below-freezing temperatures, parking in the Strip is impossible. I drive past the fresh flower stands, T-shirt vendors, sidewalk carts loaded with pad thai, meatball Parmesan subs, and sweet potato pies. Past the Italian specialty market, the antiques warehouse, the costume shop, and the largest vendor of seafood in the city. Throngs of people are squeezed on the sidewalks, spilling into the streets. Many restaurants in Pittsburgh buy their fresh produce, meat, and fish in the Strip District. On weekends, everybody else comes to the Strip to buy any number of unusual things, like Ethiopian berbere spice blend or Vietnamese sambal oelek sauce, found nowhere else in the city. When we moved here a year earlier, I was surprised to find, in the midst of what is considered a midwestern city of mostly Eastern European descendants, a Korean grocery store. How this oddity called Sam Bok exists in the heart of the Strip remains a mystery to me. How many Koreans could there be in Pittsburgh?

We drive in circles for what seems like an interminable time.

"Erin, if we don't find a spot soon, we're going home." I blow out my breath.

In the rearview mirror, I spy my daughter lounging back in her booster seat, staring out the window, her eyes glazed over. I can see her dark hair pulled back in a ballet bun with pink hair netting to match her pink leotard and pink tights. Her eyes are not as wide set as mine, and without the epicanthal folds. And her nose is more prominent, more Caucasian. But she looks like me; everyone says so.

She turns her head lazily toward me. "Come on, Mommy, we'll find one."

I raise my voice. "Erin, there are no spots! Don't you see the cars double-parked all over the place? We should go home."

Abruptly she sits up, presses her nose to the window. "Please, Mommy, please, I'll help you look. I really want to go to Sam Bok."

I am not immune to her pleading. She is seven years old. "One more time around the block. But then that's it, okay?"

"Okay," she answers quietly, so uncharacteristic of her exuberant nature.

A spot opens up and we don't even have to pay. I gloat and my daughter laughs. When we walk past the accordion player in front of Wholey's fish market, she asks for a dollar to put in his cup. A Polish polka fills the air. Laughter, snatches of conversation, and shouts of "Kettle corn, two dollars a bag!" ebb and flow around us. I wait while she runs in to pet the tomato-loving dachshund in Balcony Cookware. The wind gusts up.

We run into Sam Bok and exhale with relief. The Korean grocery store has a small sushi bar to the left of the entrance, but they don't serve sushi. Instead they have a limited selection of Korean food. We sit on

black vinyl barstools, two of only six at the counter. We are the only cus-
tomers. There are long lines outside for Korean barbecue chicken and
mung bean pancakes, but not inside. Maybe the peeling linoleum floor
deters people. Maybe it's the counter devoid of sushi. The same Korean
woman stands behind the empty glass case, waiting for our order. She
greets us in Korean. We answer hello in English.

Even though my daughter and I have come here for lunch almost
every Saturday since September, the Korean woman and I have
exchanged only a few words. Once, she asked me if I was Korean. I
answered that I was but that I didn't speak Korean well. She nodded
and walked away. Most Koreans who are fluent in their language regard
those who are not with contempt. I am resigned to this kind of attitude
and ashamed by my lack of deftness in the language of my ancestors.

One time while I was living outside of New York City, I was in a
nail salon where most of the manicurists were young Korean women.
All of them dressed in black with beige aprons. All moved with effi-
ciency behind their individual tables, their instruments organized, their
bottles of nail polish lined up by increasing vividness of color—peach,
pink, red.

A pretty, perfectly made-up young woman asked me, "Are you
Japanese?" Her English sounded stilted, her accent indicating that she
was not a native speaker.

Even Koreans think I look Japanese. I gazed at the woman sitting
across the table holding my hand and cutting my cuticles. "No."

She looked up, her winged drawn-on eyebrows raised. She waited
for my answer.

My shoulders seized. "I'm Korean," I said.

Her eyebrows seemed stuck in permanent question marks. Our eyes
met, long enough for me to see the scorn coming. She didn't even ask
if I could speak Korean.

Instead she turned to the manicurist behind her and said in Korean, *"What a pity! This Korean woman can't even speak Korean. Who has heard of such a thing?"* They laughed in unison.

I pretended I couldn't understand what she had said.

At Sam Bok, I order *udong* for my daughter, and I pick a plate of gimbap, the Korean cooked version of sushi rolls—seaweed and rice wrapped around bright-yellow pickled daikon, sautéed spinach, blanched carrot slivers, omelet egg cut in strips, and bulgogi beef. My daughter loves udong, fat white noodles in light miso broth. While the Korean woman cooks the noodles, my daughter jumps down from her barstool and makes a beeline for the candy section. She pleads with me for a sweet. I tell her, "Not until you've eaten all your noodles."

She runs around the store, shrieking about the frozen octopus and the dried shitake mushrooms. The narrow aisles crammed with red pepper paste, dried seaweed, barley tea, and ginseng root are exotic to her. The pungent scent of kimchi, impervious to refrigeration, assaults her senses. "What's that funny smell?" she keeps saying, even though she has asked this question many times before. Kimchi, spicy pickled napa cabbage, is familiar to me. A staple of my childhood, the fermenting vegetable aroma does not even register as offensive to my olfactory senses.

My daughter wonders out loud how many bottles of soy sauce are on the shelves. I tell her to sit down and eat her noodles. She obeys. She insists on picking the dark, gelatinous seaweed and the pink-and-white semicircles of fish cake out of the broth. I happily eat them for her. "They smell funny," she complains about the odor of ocean and fish. Those aromas, alien to her, are comforting to me. As her belly fills, my daughter picks up the udong noodles with her wooden chopsticks, only to drop them back into the broth again. I tell her not to play with her food. She doesn't listen. But I feel indulgent. I laugh and tell her that she's being goofy.

Then something odd happens. The Korean woman starts a conversation.

"Everything all right?" she asks in hesitant, heavily accented English.

I smile. "Everything is fine. My daughter is acting goofy, you know, silly." I speak slowly. I'm not sure she understands the word *goofy*.

She nods. "My daughter goofy too."

I'm relieved she understands me. I continue to speak slowly. "I wish she was not so goofy."

"She is good girl," the Korean woman assures me.

"Sometimes she does not behave like a good girl." I shake my head, looking at my daughter with pretend reproach.

My daughter only grins and keeps eating.

"You are too hard," the Korean woman admonishes me.

"She's not three years old, like her brother. She should behave better," I say with mock sternness.

My daughter rolls her eyes at me. "Oh, Mommy."

I feign outrage for the Korean woman. "You see that? Disrespectful!"

She laughs. "My daughter same way."

Our conversation is interrupted by two American women saying, "Excuse me."

The younger one asks if they can have yellowtail and tuna. The Korean woman says, "No sushi." The women look at her, uncomprehending. They ask what kind of sushi is available. The Korean woman says again, "No sushi." They stand at an impasse. The Korean woman pushes her fingers through her short, dark, glossy hair and nervously adjusts the glasses on her thin face. She visibly struggles to speak English before resorting to Korean. I intervene and explain to the two women that there is no sushi today because there is no sushi chef. They may have a sushi chef come summer. I've heard the Korean woman say the same thing in Korean. The women nod and leave.

"Thank you," says the Korean woman.

"I knew what you were saying. I understand Korean better than I speak it," I say, brushing off her gratitude.

"Me too. In English," she says.

"Why don't you speak in Korean? I will try to understand," I suggest.

"It is difficult for me to understand English. But it is far more difficult for me to speak English," she says in Korean.

I nod. I understand only too well.

We continue our conversation with me speaking in English and her in Korean. Although it's awkward and we end up repeating ourselves, it's still easier this way. For both of us. It reminds me of the way my mother and I used to speak. The woman I knew as articulate and highly intelligent when she spoke in Korean became a contradiction of syntax and grammar whenever she spoke English. It was particularly painful for her since she had studied English literature in translation at a teacher's college for women in Korea. Sometimes my sisters and I would interpret for her at her request. Sometimes we would do it so she wouldn't embarrass us.

"Korean is easy. English is so difficult. You have to be born here or come here as a child to be good in English." The Korean woman labors over her disfluency in a language that is not her mother tongue.

"English is hard, but Korean isn't easy."

She seems surprised. *"You understood what I said in Korean. Your Korean is much better than my English. My English is terrible."* She continues the ingrained Korean custom of elevating other people's abilities while denigrating their own.

I automatically revert to the same behavior taught to me by my mother. "My Korean is pretty bad. My mother says I can't even speak it like a six-year-old."

"My daughter was six years old when we came to America. Now she is twelve. She can understand me, but she doesn't speak well. She tells me she doesn't want to speak Korean."

"How do you feel about that?"

"I think she is a child. She wants to do only what is easy. Every Saturday she goes to Korean language school at the Korean church. She complains, but she goes."

I nod; I sympathize.

"What can I do? I am raising her in America, so she acts like an American."

"Do you have other children?"

"My son is fifteen. I have two children who both say they don't want to live in Korea."

"Do you want to live here?"

"No. My husband can get a better job in Korea after his postdoc in America. But our children will not go back, so we are staying," she says.

"You should tell your children they're very lucky to have parents like you." I know too well the way of immigrant Korean parents, desperate to give their children the best opportunities, but nostalgic for their land of origin.

Two other Korean women, probably mother and daughter by age and looks, ask her if she can prepare *yukgaejang*, a hot, spicy shredded beef soup. She apologizes and says she does not have the ingredients today. They commiserate about the scarcity of Korean food in this city and how soothing hot, spicy soup would be on this cold day. Immigrants bonding in a foreign land. I can hear the change in cadence of the Korean woman's speech. She is talking quickly and freely. She has deliberately been using simple words and sentence structure so I can understand her.

I was six years old when I left the country of my birth. I have retained much of my receptive language—I can understand most of the Korean that is spoken to me. Unfortunately, it is frozen at the comprehension and grammar of a six-year-old. And I have lost almost all of my expressive language. The previous time I tried to speak Korean, I stumbled badly. The man ringing up my purchase of a tray of Asian pears at a Korean grocery store in New Jersey asked in a joking manner if I had a houseful of people to eat them. I smiled and tried to answer, but I used words that made no sense. I stood humiliated while he berated me that it was shameful for a Korean not to know how to speak Korean. He looked at me in disgust.

"How can you be Korean?"

After that incident, I refused to speak Korean. On the rare occasions that I went to a Korean restaurant, I stopped returning the customary greeting and bow. I simply answered in English. It was easier to tolerate their silent contempt than face my outright failure. So I am wary, but the Korean woman is not judgmental, not disparaging. In fact she tries to encourage me. She tells me repeatedly that my Korean is very good. As we continue to talk, I gain confidence. I even try to say some words in Korean, phrases like *I know* and *I understand.*

My daughter looks at me wide-eyed. "I didn't know you could speak Korean."

She doesn't remember the times when she was an infant and I would sing to her in Korean. A song my mother used to sing when we lived in Korea, Uganda, Virginia, and New Jersey. The first two verses of that song—about memories of a childhood home in the verdant mountains of Korea, a beautiful village of abundant flowers and weeping willows on the banks of a river—are indelibly imprinted on me. My mother told me that I had sung that same song for my first-grade class on the day I left *Rhee Rah*, my school in Seoul.

"Where is your mother?" the Korean woman asks.

I should have known she would ask me about my mother, but I am still surprised when she does. Koreans love talking about their children, their families. If you asked any Korean what the most important thing in life is, you would probably receive only one word in answer: *gahjok.* Family.

"My mother lives in New Jersey."

"Do you see her often?"

I hesitate.

My mother and I are estranged. I have not seen or spoken to her in years, except for my youngest sister's wedding last year. Two words—hello, goodbye—really don't count. I find it difficult to talk about my mother with even my closest friends, never mind a complete stranger, a Korean at that. But my daughter is no longer sitting next to me. She has disappeared, lost in the rows of soy sauce, brown rice vinegar, sesame oil. I do not have to be careful with my words.

"I haven't seen my mother in years."

The Korean woman looks shocked. *"Why?"*

"She's not happy with me. She's angry," I say, trying to keep my tone light.

The Korean woman stops hand-rolling the seaweed-enshrouded gimbap. She looks at me in consternation. *"Your mother is not angry with you. You misunderstand her intentions."*

I shake my head. "I know she's angry. She doesn't speak to me or my sisters. She says we all failed her—we married American men, not Korean men." I do not elaborate. How do I begin to explain that we failed her in so many other ways? That we were not the jangsohn she prayed for, merely daughters who had not made good marriages.

"But you have children. She must see her grandchildren." The Korean woman's disbelief will not be assuaged.

"She has five grandchildren. She sees none of them." I can hear the bitterness in my voice.

The Korean woman looks at me with kindness. *"Your mother is Korean. You must be the one to make the effort. You must go to her house and bring your children."*

"What if she won't let me in?" I ask, doubtful about this course of action. I have gone to my mother's house before and knocked on her door. I have been rejected and refused entry.

The Korean woman shakes her head. *"She may appear angry, but she will be happy to see you. She wants to see her grandchildren. The second time you go will be easier, and the third time even better. She loves you. You must try.*"

I remain skeptical. "I think you are mistaken."

She will not be dissuaded. "*I speak the truth. You will see. There is no reason for me to lie. I have nothing to gain.*"

She is right; she has nothing to gain. But I am tired. I have spent my life begging my mother. I balk at the thought of asking for one more thing, but I do not say that to the Korean woman. Perhaps I cannot deny the possibility that my mother and I will speak, one day. When I can get past my guilt and her recriminations, and she can forgive what she perceives as my failures.

An occasional customer straggles into Sam Bok, ordering bulgogi or *bibimbap*, popular Korean dishes of beef barbecue and mixed vegetables and rice. Mostly to go. One older man has chosen to eat here. He wipes his napkin across his mouth, stands up, and pulls out his wallet. He turns to me and asks for the cost of his dish. I tell him I don't know. I search for the Korean woman. But she has moved to the far end of the kitchen to chop carrots and yellow daikon. I can shout, "Excuse me!" But that seems rude. I get up from my barstool and walk to the entrance of the cooking area. I push aside the blue-and-white cloth curtain.

I call out, "*Ahjumma?*"

She turns around. She smiles. "*It is true, you know Korean very well.*"

I shake my head, saying only that a customer needs help. I do not tell her that the word Koreans use to refer to a female who is unrelated to them only just occurred to me. I knew instinctively that I could not use her name—not that I knew her name. The word *ahjumma* surfaced as I struggled with the etiquette of how I should address her. It arrived from the depths of memory I did not know I possessed.

Ahjumma literally means "aunt." But it is the word Koreans use for women who are not related to them because we do not ever use such generic terms like *aunt* or *uncle* to refer to members of our own family. Because Koreans use such precise terminology like *emo*, mother's sister, or *gomo*, father's sister, instead of aunt, in addressing or referring to those specific family members, ahjumma is what I should call this woman if I want to be polite. But that is not to say I am being deferential. Deference is reserved for elder relatives or prominent community members, not shopkeepers or cooks, as my mother once instructed me in the social order of Korean class.

I continue to practice my halting Korean with Ahjumma, and although I am dismal, she compliments me. She is Korean, brought up to be unfailingly polite. But she is far more than just a polite Korean. Instead of hiding in her insular world, she has chosen to reach beyond strict Korean hierarchies and befriend an outsider caught between two cultures. I want to cry. Instead I take a deep breath and let my lungs fill with air. I am grateful I do not have to feel ashamed anymore.

My daughter, long finished with her noodles, has been wandering the store. She comes back impatient to leave. She has picked out her dessert—pretzel sticks coated with strawberry-flavored icing. The pink cone-shaped container with pictures of strawberries and Korean writing appeals to her. Ahjumma and I stop our conversation. In Korean, Ahjumma tells my daughter that she is pretty. I translate and prompt my daughter to say thank you, which she shouts as she runs out of Sam Bok. Telling her to wait for me, I pay for our food and leave a tip in the white Styrofoam cup. Ahjumma tries to give the money back to me, saying it is too much for so little effort. I wave her off as I walk quickly to the door. I stop and turn around. She is looking at me. I smile and say the customary farewell in Korean as I bow. She nods in approval as she returns my bow.

I step back into the cold and meld with the crowd.

Chapter 11
A Successful Doctor

Gwangju, 1960. In beautiful Western-style dresses, my mother and my grandmother walk down a narrow alley lined with traditional Korean houses with charcoal-blue tile roofs. Because of my grandfather's wealth and status as a banker, my mother and grandmother do not wear hanboks, women's traditional dress. They speak softly about my mother's upcoming wedding—the white dress, the beautiful flowers. My mother's voice has an excited uplift; my grandmother's is more cautious. They stop at a thick wooden door with massive black metal rings as handles. They enter a traditional courtyard, the serenity of silence and miniature trees greeting them. Easing off their shoes, they step up to a pine platform, slide open a door made of hanji paper and light wood, and kneel on crimson embroidered cushions on the bamboo floor. A black lacquered table separates them from the fortune-teller in a red hanbok.

The woman reaches for my mother's pale, uncalloused hands, turns the palms upright.

My mother's hands tremble. "What do you see?"

The woman's face becomes blank; her fingers dig into vulnerable flesh.

My mother's shoulders stiffen.

"You will have a son," the woman intones.

My mother exhales her long-held breath.

"Your children will bring wealth and prestige to your family. One will become a doctor," the fortune-teller says.

My mother smiles.

⁓

"Were you a successful doctor?" asks the young woman sitting next to me.

Her blue eyes and peaches-and-cream complexion are so fresh and innocent. But her question makes my shoulders pull forward, my neck go rigid. It's December 2004, and I am riding a city bus to my undergraduate English class at the University of Pittsburgh. At almost forty years old, I am back in college—and, no less, at the same institution where I was an assistant professor almost a year ago. I am taking Senior Seminar in Creative Nonfiction, with twenty-two-year-olds about to graduate college, and Introduction to Poetry with eighteen-year-old freshmen.

Were you a successful doctor?

The evening is near balmy, and the air that seeps through the cracked-open window smells clean and crisp. It feels more like spring than winter. And the words *successful doctor* sound oddly familiar. The young woman's question echoes back into the far chambers of my memory. I stare out the window as the bus propels its way down Forbes Avenue, heading toward the Cathedral of Learning and its distinct gothic spires. Then I remember: *Maritza's grandmother.*

Maritza and I met through an introduction to computers class in high school. She was a senior and I, a sophomore. Our paths had not crossed before. Maritza was part of the popular crowd; I was pursuing the honors track. Our final class project involved several groups of students competing to design a computer program of nonrepeating random numbers in a series of four. I'd been working on the project with Maritza and Bernadette, another sophomore, for weeks when Maritza invited us for Sunday dinner to complete our assignment.

On that clear spring evening, Bernadette and I chatted about our upcoming summer jobs as we wended up Boulevard East along the Hudson River. Maritza lived in a doorman building; Bernadette and I had to be announced before we were allowed to take the elevator to her apartment. A diminutive woman with gray-streaked black hair answered the door.

"Please, come in," she said in accented English with lyrical Spanish undertones.

We walked into a living room decorated in beige and silver, with a wall of windows facing the New York skyline. Freshly cut white lilies artfully arranged in a crystal vase sat on the glass and gold chrome coffee table.

"Thank you for inviting us to dinner," I said.

"You are welcome in this house," she replied as she touched us both, guiding us onto a cream leather sofa. "I am grandmother to Maritza."

"Oh, you have a beautiful apartment. What a fantastic view!" Bernadette gestured effusively at the Empire State Building. It seemed close enough to touch.

Maritza's grandmother nodded. She seemed distracted. Instead of looking out the window, she was staring at me. Her small dark eyes, in a gently wrinkled face, were piercing but kind. "Korean?" she said, not so much as a question, but as an acknowledgment.

I was surprised she guessed right. "Yes."

"You want to be a doctor?" Maritza's grandmother asked. "You will be a successful doctor," she said without hesitation.

"Thank you," I said quietly, disconcerted.

"What about me?" Bernadette asked with a nervous laugh, her round face earnest and eager. She almost pleaded, "I want to be a doctor too."

Maritza's grandmother smiled. "You will be good at what you become."

Bernadette smiled back, reassured.

"Hey, guys!" Maritza called out as she entered the spacious living room. "My grandmother came from Puerto Rico for my graduation. Isn't that great?"

Maritza, a statuesque brunette, motioned for us to follow her into the adjoining dining room. Dominating the room was an enormous glass table with sleek white chairs, furniture popular in the 1980s. Platters of fragrant arroz con pollo, garlic shrimp, rice and beans, and fried sweet plantains seemed suspended in midair above plush carpeting. Bernadette and I met the rest of Maritza's family. Gregarious and affectionate, in contrast to my Korean family, they enveloped me in welcome. Dinner was a cacophony of teasing and laughter. After the last bite of flan with *café con leche* was consumed, Maritza, Bernadette, and I worked on our computer program.

When I saw Maritza on Monday, instead of talking about our project, she made a strange announcement: "My grandmother wants you to know that not only will you become a doctor, but you will marry one. And she says you will meet him across a table."

"Oh, Maritza, why did you have to tell your grandmother I wanted to be a doctor?"

"I never said anything to my grandmother," Maritza said.

∽

"Why does it have to rain today?" my mother would typically fret when I was in high school. She would push back the white lace curtains, looking mournfully out the window.

"It's only a light rain," I would say.

"The fates are against us," she would say.

"We'll be in the car," I would say.

"Why are we so unlucky?" she would ask.

It was only a trip to the grocery store.

By nature, my mother was a superstitious person. Being Korean made it worse. She had been raised in a culture invested in the mythology of ghosts, reincarnation, fate, destiny. My mother believed in lucky and unlucky numbers—three and seven were lucky; four was unlucky. My mother believed in premonitions and prophecies. Fate and destiny were not vague, abstract concepts, but tangible, foreseeable events bound to happen. When my mother was about to marry, my grandmother took her to see a psychic. My mother assured me that it was customary in Korea for a woman to have her future divined by a fortune-teller before her wedding. The soothsayer told my mother she would be blessed with good fortune—both a son and a doctor in the family. My mother did everything in her power to make those fateful predictions come true.

Maritza graduated from high school and went to college. I never saw her or her grandmother again. I heard from an old classmate that Bernadette became a nurse. I became a pediatrician. My ex-husband was also a physician. We were introduced at a bar, a hangout popular with students near the medical school campus. I can't remember if we met across a table.

I never told my mother what Maritza's grandmother said that balmy night. At age fifteen, I was unnerved by the idea that I was destined to be the doctor in my mother's fortune, foretold by a woman I never met, years before I was born. Can a girl's life really be mapped out by her mother's dreams? I became a doctor because my parents wanted me to be one. And even when I wanted to leave medicine, I believed I was *supposed* to be one. It was easier to have someone else, something else, decide what I should do with my life. I resigned myself to fate. After all, my fate, in a way, was sealed before I was born.

❡

Were you a successful doctor?

What does it mean to be a successful doctor? I knew a successful doctor once—James Oleske, the physician who devoted his life to caring for children with HIV/AIDS. An extraordinary human being. A hero. Homer's Odysseus without the flaws. Shakespeare's Henry V on the battlefield of preventable infectious diseases. Austen's Mr. Knightley transported from *Emma* into the pediatrician world. By that measure, I was not a successful doctor. Introverted by nature, I had forced myself for years to wear the persona of an exuberant extrovert—plastering a smile on my face, greeting my patients with false cheer: "Hi! How are you doing?" Pediatricians are supposed to be warm and fuzzy. Not awkward or painfully shy.

On the bus to my creative writing class, I shift in my seat. I wiggle the toes in my right foot to ward off numbness. My hand automatically reaches back—a pattern established after my car accident, whenever I feel a twinge in my spine—and I massage the flesh around my right iliac crest.

I remember the times during my pediatric training when my back ached from so many hours on my feet, the fatigue, the mental exhaustion. In the early hours of the morning, pediatric residents used to gather in the lounge or at a nursing station to write notes or debrief about an admission, having given up on the idea of sleep for the night. In those moments, when we were so sleep deprived and vulnerable, we spoke openly, a rarity in the guarded world of tense trainees. We talked about our lives outside the hospital and bemoaned the lost possibilities. The most bantered-about question was "What would you have done if you hadn't gone to medical school?" One resident said he would have been a plumber. Another resident announced that he would have been perfectly happy working at a desk in a cubicle. Yet another resident confessed that she loved creating art with sugar icing. If she had the chance again, she said, she would become a cake baker. I always said the same thing: an English professor at a small New England college. I didn't grow up in New England; I hadn't majored in English. Yet every time I said it, the more certain I felt that was how my life should have been.

I remember the cinder block garage attached to our two-bedroom house in Kampala, Uganda, and the books piled high in haphazard stacks against the damp gray. As soon as I could read in English, I started to devour the numerous volumes. I began with Ladybird books and quickly moved on to *The Secret Seven* by Enid Blyton. The way I chose which books to read was whimsical at best—the illustration on the cover, the style of the font, the eloquence of the title. I read *Common Sense* by Thomas Paine because my eight-year-old self fancied the stylized black lettering of the title and the ornate, gilt-framed portrait of a man in a powdered wig and white cravat. I picked *Jane Eyre* by Charlotte Brontë because the picture on the cover was irresistible—a young woman with a candle in her hand, illuminating the dark. I still can't remember a word of *Common Sense*. But for years I had nightmares about Mr. Rochester's mad and pyrotechnic wife locked up in the attic.

The smell of mold and paper still evokes the pleasure of discovering different universes, different families. Those books, abandoned by a British expat who probably didn't want to spend the money to ship them to a new home, ignited my lifelong love of literature. When we settled in America, first in Virginia, then New Jersey, I took refuge in libraries. I would sit surrounded by books, my head bent over open binding, wandering around imagined worlds.

Were you a successful doctor?

I sway from side to side on the rattling bus, staring out the window at the well-manicured lawns of Squirrel Hill. I avoid looking at the curious young woman. I wonder: *What am I doing?* Why leave a career in which I was respected by patients and liked by young doctors in training, and taught at some of the best children's hospitals in the country? A career that most people say is a calling. Yet I hear the siren of literature: Shakespeare, Austen, Morrison, Hong Kingston, Didion.

Were you a successful doctor?

I struggle between truth and facade. Finally I say, "I was a competent doctor. But it wasn't my passion."

She smiles at me.

I smile back.

She tells me about her Shakespeare class and her decision to become an English major. I tell her how much I love the language of Shakespeare. I don't tell her I've applied to Pitt's MFA program in creative nonfiction as a middle-aged woman. I don't tell her that I'm changing my fate.

On the speeding bus, I stretch my spine tall. I take a deep breath. I exhale.

Chapter 12
The Cranes

I feel strangely relieved but still thwarted when my mother doesn't answer my knock on her door. I try to block out all emotion. I hold my breath. We knock again. Ring the bell insistently. I stare at the peephole of the blank white door, willing darkness to hint that she is inside looking out. I see not a flicker of shadow. I hear no evidence of surreptitious movement. No aromas of kimchi stew simmering, not even the wet scent of rice. Maybe she is not home.

It is summer 2005, and my daughter and I are standing outside my mother's apartment in Edison, New Jersey. My mother lives in an "active adult community," a collection of one- and two-bedroom housing units for seniors. Her apartment is on the third floor, the last one on the left from a bank of elevators, down a long hallway lit by wall sconces shaped like champagne flutes. All the entrances to the apartments are tucked into beige alcoves. My mother has personalized hers with silk white roses and purple lilies of the valley in porcelain vases perched on a ledge, and a welcome mat in front of her door. Even if I didn't know the number, I would have recognized the stamp of her personality—no matter the circumstances, one must keep up appearances.

My sister was right. I could see the doubt on Susan's face, as she raised her eyebrows and tilted her head ever so slightly, in response to my deliberately nonchalant statement that I was going to visit our mother. "Did you tell her you're coming? You know what Mom's like." But our mother has banned telephones from her home, and there was no time to write. All the signs have warned me this is a doomed pilgrimage. But I am stubborn; I have come anyway.

The last time I saw my mother was more than a year earlier. I had flown in from Pittsburgh to attend a family meeting with my three sisters and the social worker of the Carrier Clinic, an acute psychiatric-care facility. My mother had been committed involuntarily. And I still remember darkness in the windows, framed by red-painted wood, as the phone rang late one night, the shrill sound echoing in my tall-ceilinged kitchen. On the other end, Susan crying so hard her words had been barely intelligible.

"Mom tried to kill herself," my sister said.

"What?" I stared at ghostly wisteria branches swaying in the night breeze. *I am in a nightmare. I will wake up.*

"Mom tried to kill herself."

The sound of her sobs, the waxing and waning of mucus and congestion, transmitted through the wire and was amplified in the still air of my kitchen.

"We were arguing in the car because she wanted to go to H Mart and I told her it was closed. She yelled at me and called me a liar and a terrible daughter. I tried to calm her down. But she wouldn't stop. I pulled over. Before I knew what was happening, she ran onto Route 1, screaming that she didn't want to live anymore." Susan's voice cracked as she said *live* and then dissolved after *anymore*.

The psychiatrist's diagnosis of my mother: major depression with psychotic features.

As a physician, I understood what that meant. As a daughter, I had no idea what was going on with my mother. She had hoarded newspapers, magazines, supermarket circulars, Macy's catalogs, stacked almost to the ceiling. She would not flush the toilet for fear the government could hear her thoughts. How could I reconcile myself to the fact that my mother stored her stool in jars?

In the conference room of the Carrier Clinic, across an institutional table, I had faced my mother. I held my body rigid, my shoulders clenched. "Mom, please stay. You need help," I said. She did not cry. She said, *Do you think I'm crazy?* And in her eyes, a sorrow I could not face. My heart squeezed so hard it felt as if my chest had caved in. My mother voluntarily committed herself for six more weeks of treatment.

After the Carrier Clinic, my sister Sophia cosigned a lease with my mother on a two-bedroom apartment near Sophia's house. Immediately upon moving in, my mother complained. The apartment was too small, the price was too high, and most disturbing to her, my sisters had spare keys. Intensely private and paranoid, she could not abide by the idea that anyone, especially her daughters, could have access to her life. When my sisters, who all lived nearby, came to check up on her, she refused to answer the door. Because they had the power to open the door, they no longer waited outside, as we all used to when she lived in her own house—a house that had fallen down around her in spite of her studious oblivion. As soon as the one-year lease was up on the cosigned apartment, my mother found this active adult community without my sisters' help or approval. Only she has the keys to this place.

I have really come to get the Cranes. For years, a massive painting of cranes hung in the living room of my mother's house. Placed between two windows, setting sunlight danced on the birds' wings, deepening hues, adding texture. Deep, verdant mountainsides and black-and-white cranes with scarlet-streaked heads created a stark yet lush picture. My mother, who normally detested cleaning, diligently dusted the painting, cleaned the glass, and oiled the wood frame surrounding the Cranes. Remnants of a home, a country she had forsaken so many years ago. Large in scale and presence, the Cranes steadfastly survived the madness of my mother's house.

Cranes, those fragile appearing but hardy birds with impossibly thin stalks for legs, are symbols of good fortune, longevity, and loyalty to Koreans. Walk into any Korean home and you will find a crane somewhere. Standing, flying, still. In a deeply superstitious culture, any image can be construed as lucky. But I have always loved cranes—unconsciously, instinctively. Graceful yet strong. Delicate but enduring. Perhaps my mother is right. This love of cranes is embedded in my DNA, the result of thousands of years of pure Korean ancestry. Sometimes, one cannot fight one's genes.

When my sisters and I sold our mother's house, we divided the furniture: Susan took the Korean black lacquered tables and a Louis XIV replica wing chair; Sophia garnered the Queen Anne china cabinet and the Steinway piano; Clara claimed my mother's British colonial mahogany bed, highboy, and armoire. But I wanted only the Cranes. Susan has been storing the Cranes in her garage for almost a year now. "Come for them anytime. There's no rush," she said. But she is moving to Hawaii in a week, and I pretended that it was on a whim I came to visit her and to get the Cranes. She has offered to keep them until her house sells, which could be months from now. But I think it is finally time to get them. And to see my mother.

Because I could not face doing this by myself, I took my daughter out of summer camp to accompany me. I am not above using a nine-year-old as a shield. An impromptu visit with her cousins excited her, and she thanked me instead. I warned her that we were also seeing Halmoni, her Korean grandmother. She shrugged, made no comment. We headed out of Pittsburgh on a sweltering summer day, the air conditioning broken in my car. I did not know how much I would regret my words: "It's okay. We'll manage." I had heard the weatherman say that this was the start of a heat wave. But I did not listen. For six and a half hours, we sweated across Pennsylvania into New Jersey.

⁓৩

While I was driving from Susan's house to my mother's new apartment, I avoided thinking about her reaction to my visit by obsessing over what I should bring as a housewarming gift. I did not have the foresight to buy something before beginning this journey. *What should I offer her?* As the miles passed on Route 1 in New Jersey, I began to panic and looked closely at every strip mall by the side of the highway. Nothing seemed appropriate— there were only hair salons, car dealerships, movie theaters, McDonald's. When I saw the entrance to Woodbridge Mall, I became desperate.

"Hey, Erin, what do you think we should bring Halmoni?"

No answer.

"Erin, are you listening?"

"Yes, Mommy?"

"What should we give Halmoni? It's nice to bring a gift when you visit, especially when it's a new place."

She giggled uncomfortably. "I don't know."

"Think of something, okay?"

"She's your mother!" Inherent in my daughter's tone was the implication that I should know what my mother might want or need.

"Erin, please, just help me out here," I pleaded.

"Okay, but I really don't know Halmoni. I remember only seeing her two or three times when I was little. And I only remember those times because there're pictures. Do you remember the one when I was only a year old? The one where I'm sitting next to a doll carriage playing with Emily's doll, and Halmoni is sitting next to me wearing this enormous white hat? She's my grandmother, so I love her. And I'm sure she loves me. But I don't really know what she likes or doesn't like. You're her daughter. Shouldn't you know?"

I remain conflicted about how articulate my daughter is. At age nine, she has eloquently explained why she cannot recommend a gift for her grandmother. This girl—who started talking at nine months with

"Elmo," who blew past two-word sentences at twelve months and could enunciate "armadillo" so clearly at fifteen months that my pediatrician colleagues would not believe me until she said it for them in person— has with just a few words exposed my failure to understand my mother.

Instead of answering my daughter's question, I grunted something noncommittal. I followed the signs to Woodbridge Mall, then veered away and took the exit ramp out. What could I possibly buy at the mall that my mother would need—a neck massager from Brookstone? A hat from Bloomingdale's? What do I buy for a woman who has lost her mind?

After running out of options, I stop at a strip mall near her apartment and buy Boston Kremes from Dunkin' Donuts, her favorites. I realize that there is nothing I can buy her in exchange for the Cranes, which are too large to fit in her apartment. But it feels like a betrayal. I tell myself that I'm safeguarding them for her. I tell myself that someday when she is well, we can start anew, and the Cranes will be where they belong.

I stand at my mother's door, not knowing what to do. I have picked the last day of my trip to see her. Before I made the drive, Susan said, "Don't expect much. Mom's been there only three weeks. But she's back to not answering her door."

I knock again, my knuckles rapping on solid white blankness. The hollow sound echoes in the long, empty corridor. "Mom, it's me. And Erin is here too," I say. My voice trembles, and I have to stop it from breaking. I swallow hard, the back of my throat arid and airless.

"Are you sure she's home?" My daughter looks up at me, her brown eyes wide and clear.

"Erin, I don't know." Impatience floods my voice. I lower my hands to my sides, but they remain frozen in tight curls, my fingernails digging into the flesh of my palms.

"If she was home, she would answer the door, right?" My daughter says this almost like a statement.

The only words that ring in my head: *I shouldn't have come.*

The last conversation I had with my mother was over the phone, after she left the Carrier Clinic. I had called because of what Susan said to me: "She heard the day we met with the social worker that you aren't working as a doctor. She keeps asking me about it." Initially I tried to dismiss this as nonsense, but my sister's words plagued me. Finally I picked up the phone.

After multiple rings, a hesitant voice said in English, "Hello?"

"Mom?"

"Oh, it's you." My mother's voice changed in tone as she continued to speak in English.

I squeezed my eyes shut. "How are you doing, Mom?"

"Okay," my mother said tersely.

My shoulders pulled forward. "Susan said you're worried about me."

Silence on her end.

I tried again. "I'm fine. I'm not working as a pediatrician because I want to stay home with my kids."

I could not stop lying to my mother. It had become a habit. It was easier for me to lie than to face her scorn. I could not tell her that I stopped practicing pediatrics because of such entangled reasons, like I was turning forty and knew I wasn't happy being a doctor; I was injured in a car accident and lived with chronic pain; I was burned out from taking care of poor kids in the inner city for little money and no support from an institution that called me an assistant professor of pediatrics. I was afraid to tell my mother that I was going back to graduate school to get a degree in creative writing. I knew she wanted me to continue being a doctor.

Maybe I should have told her I was worried about *her*, but we didn't have that kind of relationship.

Still only silence on her end.

"Mom?"

"Okay, okay," she said, her voice dismissive.

Again I tried. "Please don't worry about me."

"Fine." She hung up the phone.

I stood in my kitchen, dial tone to my ear.

Of course, I could not know our trip out to my mother's apartment in New Jersey would only be rivaled by the equally difficult trip back. While driving home through a deluge in the Appalachian Mountains, I will join a line of cars, with hazard lights blinking, crawling at twenty miles per hour on the Pennsylvania Turnpike. For an interminable time, my windshield wipers will sway furiously from side to side, unable to erase the sheets of rain. Although it will be steaming inside because of the broken air conditioning, I will keep the windows open only a crack, afraid it will rain on the Cranes wedged in the back seat. The water will come sideways into my car, missing my sticky face but landing squarely on the Cranes. Then the oil light will burn orange in warning. That is when I will give up. I will crank the windows all the way down—if the Cranes are going to get wet, then we might as well all get soaked. Ironically, my actions will direct the rain away from the Cranes. My daughter will laugh out loud when water hits her arm. "Mommy, this is *way* cool!" she will say, her hair plastered to her forehead, her face dewy with droplets, not of perspiration, but of rain.

She will be right. The water will be cool, calming in the middle of that maelstrom. I will stop clenching the steering wheel, no longer hearing the whisper of my mother's voice berating me, no longer imagining the Cranes flooded and ruined but imagining them alive, taking flight, the rain beating off their backs.

Chapter 13
Mother Tongue

Mom! There's a woman asking for you. I think she's Korean!" my nine-year-old daughter whispers loudly, her eyes wide.

She thrusts the cordless phone into my hands and stands as if rooted to an imaginary spot in our mint-green kitchen. She follows me with her eyes. I lean my elbows on the butcher-block island in the center of the kitchen and focus my gaze on the wood grain. It's a return phone call from the Korean Central Church of Pittsburgh, which I had called asking about Korean language classes for adults. My mother's suicide attempt has triggered a yearning in me to relearn the language of my birth country, the language I must have heard in my mother's womb, the language that was, at one time, my native tongue. I realize that without my mother, my last connection to the Korean language will be gone.

When I left Seoul, I lost my Korean. In Uganda, linguistic experts told my parents to stop speaking our mother tongue and speak only English if they wanted their daughters to be fluent. My parents listened, and the loss of a culture began. My home became a silent vacuum as my parents, who were uncomfortable speaking English, chose not to talk to us rather than stumble and sound foolish. Eventually, our communications reflected the classic stiltedness of many immigrant families—my parents would speak to us in Korean; my sisters and I would answer in English. And in marrying a white man, I shifted further from my mother tongue, forgetting what little I remembered from my childhood.

"Hello?" I say, my hand gripping the black handset.

The standard Korean greeting, *"Ahnyeong haseyo,"* is the response from a cheerful female voice.

"I am sorry, but I cannot speak Korean." I enunciate clearly, slowing my speech. My shoulders pull forward.

"Please, do not trouble yourself. I understand English, but it is so poor I must speak in Korean," she apologizes in turn, like a typical Korean woman.

"I am the one who should be sorry. Even though I am Korean, I cannot speak Korean," I say, my head bowed.

"Please do not worry," she says, trying to soothe me. *"I am Mrs. Lee, the pastor's wife. I am sorry, but we have Korean language school only for children. Not adults. On Saturdays, our volunteer teachers give instruction for two hours in the morning. Afterward, the children have snack time, and then an activity of their choice—Korean dance, tae kwon do, arts and crafts, or sewing."*

"I'm sorry I bothered you." My shoulders sink.

"Do you have children? Would you like to put your children in Korean language school?" she says.

"My daughter is nine and my son is five. I'm not sure if they would want to go to Korean school. I can't even read or write Korean," I say, my skin flushing with shame. I know Korean teachers give prodigious amounts of homework, and my children will be lost.

"We will help your children. And when you learn Korean, you can help them too. Do you know they have Korean language classes at the University of Pittsburgh?" she says.

"Really?" I straighten my spine, push away from the kitchen island. I hadn't thought of the possibility that Korean would be offered at Pitt.

Twenty years ago, when I was in college, Korean language wasn't an option. But I wonder if I would have taken it. My mother had suggested that I go to Korea the summer of my junior year in college, but I chose an English literature and theater program in London instead. My love of Shakespeare burned so brightly that my twenty-year-old self was convinced I had lived in Elizabethan England in another lifetime.

And now I'm about to embark on my delayed dream to be a writer, an MFA candidate in creative writing at the University of Pittsburgh. But I withhold this fact from Mrs. Lee. I'm still not comfortable telling people that I left the practice of medicine, still feeling guilt that I left what some people call a "noble" profession.

"Why don't you call the university? We can start your children in our Saturday classes next week. We will do whatever is necessary to make them feel welcome. We want to help them learn the language of their mother," she says with fervor, as though her willingness can overcome my lack of proficiency in the language that should be my mother tongue.

I am not used to kindness from a Korean woman. I thank Mrs. Lee and tell her I will think about what she has said. I hang up the phone.

"Are we going to Korean school?" My daughter looks up at me, her face a mixture of wonder and doubt.

"I don't know," I say.

For a moment, there is silence.

"I want to learn Korean!" my daughter shouts.

"Me too!" My son mimics his older sister.

"Hold on, we need to talk about this before we make any decisions," I say.

"We can all learn Korean together!" My daughter refuses to let my caution dampen her enthusiasm. She grabs her brother's hands. They dance around the kitchen, their arms and legs flinging out in abandon, their small bodies unrestrained.

After I send them off to play in the backyard, I sit on a kitchen chair, looking out onto the back porch. Wisteria twist and climb around wood posts painted red and cream, the soft summer breeze ruffling purple blossoms. I am grateful for Mrs. Lee and what she said about my children learning *"the language of their mother."* Korean used to be my mother tongue. When I was in first grade, in Seoul, I learned to read and write Hangul proficiently in only one month, according to my mother. She had been astonished because, as the third child, I was so shy and quiet she had thought I was not very bright. Now I cannot read one word in Korean. I can't even remember the basics of the alphabet.

I think back to the conversation I had with the Korean woman at Sam Bok last year. Inside that small Korean grocery store in the Strip District, I had spoken about my mother's isolation and mental illness, about the estrangement between my mother and me. Things I rarely told anyone. The Korean shopkeeper had been kind, as kind as the pastor's wife just now on the phone. Maybe it's possible that I don't have to feel shame around a Korean woman. Maybe I can relearn the language of my ancestors and also help my children learn the language of their people.

I stand at the bus stop, burrowing into my gray peacoat, muttering to myself. *Too much. Very much. Really.* I cannot pronounce these words in Korean. My tongue trips and stumbles over the same words I am sure I used as a child. Even though I can hear my mother saying them in the faint echo chamber of my memory, I cannot reproduce those same sounds. They are foreign to me now, tongue twisters instead of everyday language.

Korean is considered an Altaic language, along with Hungarian, Finnish, Turkish, Estonian, and Mongolian. Vastly different in sentence structure and phonology from English, a Germanic language, Korean is one of the most difficult languages for native English speakers to learn. And vice versa. Koreans remain confounded by the subject-verb-object construction of English, because in Korean either the subject or the object can begin a sentence. It only matters that a sentence ends with a verb. Articles do not exist in Korean: there is no such thing as *a* or *the* before a noun. And there's no difference in the pronunciation or spelling of the singular or plural form of a noun—it's implicit in the context of the sentence, whether you are talking about one book or many books. Prepositions are also not important in Korean and are frequently omitted in speech, because it's understood that you are sitting *on* a chair, not over or underneath it.

Phonemes produced in Korean often do not exist in English. The first *g* in Gwangju, the city where I was born, is pronounced like a combination of *g* and *k*, a sound that is difficult, if not impossible, for native English speakers to emanate. Twin consonants and double vowels, common in Korean, bewilder the tongues of non-native speakers. And there is no *f* sound in Korean. Borrowed words from English, like *buffet* and *fighting*, are pronounced "bu-pay" and "hi-ting" in Korean. Complicating matters further, Korean is a syllable-timed language, where there is no emphasis placed on any part of a word. For instance, the word *camera* would be pronounced "*ka*-mera" in English, with the accent on the first syllable, but "kah-meh-rah" in Korean, with no emphasis on any single syllable. But Korean is not monotonous. Rather, it is musical—no staccato harshness, just gentle dips of intonation and slight changes in inflection. Almost poetic in nature. Even when I could barely speak it, Korean always sounded beautiful to me.

Entirely engrossed in my attempts to speak Korean, I miss the Asian woman standing next to me.

"Excuse me," she says.

Startled, I turn around.

"Are you speaking Korean?" The woman, with long black hair and black-framed glasses, gestures at the paper in my hand.

"I'm studying for a test. I take Korean classes at Pitt," I say, my eyes watchful, my shoulders tense.

"That's great! I'm Korean. Is there anything I can help you with?" she says.

The kindness of strangers shatters something inside me. The shards embed in my heart, seep into the marrow of my bones, spread like heat in my belly. I want to cry. Instead I take a deep breath and hold it. I pretend to this solicitous Korean woman that I am fine. I pretend that it is not humiliating that my tongue won't twist, won't slide, won't make the sounds that are words instead of gibberish. I want to hide from the brutal truth that I am no longer a native speaker.

Because my mother didn't teach me Korean, I am learning it from a Turkish woman. She instructs all the Korean language classes at the University of Pittsburgh. I was skeptical when I read her bio on the East Asian languages and literatures home page looking for the Korean professor's email address. Born and raised in Turkey, she studied Korean in college and pursued it at Seoul National University for three years at the graduate level. She received her doctorate in Korean language and linguistics from the University of Hawaii. I was still skeptical. But Ebru proves me wrong with her impeccable Korean. She is generous in allowing me to join her class, even though it's officially full. I think she pities me—I saw her grimace when I told her I stopped being a doctor. I wonder if she thinks that I made a mistake. What an odd choice it is to pursue writing so late in life. Does she think I'm crazy for leaving a stable career, a known entity? Will she be surprised I sometimes think exactly that? At age forty, I'm the oldest student in the class, closer in age to Ebru than to the rest of my classmates.

The kids in Korean class, only eighteen and nineteen years old, remind me of younger, different versions of me. Yet not me. Linda, who was born in this country, dutifully went to Korean school as a child and is taking this class for an "easy A." But she says, "I'm the whitest

Korean you'll ever meet," as she gives me a sideways glance through her blue-colored contact lenses.

Erica was adopted by white American parents when she was a toddler. She has no memory of Korea. She is majoring in economics and speaks amicably of Korea's role in the global economy. She seems to bear no grudge toward the country that gave her away. Extroverted and articulate, she mounted an energetic campaign to be a member of the student senate and won. In her first year of learning Korean, she took over as president of the Korean Student Association.

It seems that Erica even dresses the part. "She wears colors and patterns just like the women in Korea," Ebru says.

"You mean the high heels and the pink satin raincoat that no sensible person would ever wear in the rain?"

Ebru laughs. "Yes! But that's not it."

"She has a lot of Korean American friends. Maybe she's imitating them," I suggest.

Ebru shakes her head. "Koreans in America dress like Americans. Erica is different. She chooses colors and coordinates her outfits like she is Korean."

How does a girl raised in one country dress with the cultural instincts of another, albeit the country of her birth? Does she even know that she acts Korean? As a former assistant professor of pediatrics, I am fascinated by the deep seeding of memory and the inheritance of qualities we didn't even know we possessed. A study involving Dutch speakers who were Korean adoptees suggests that memory of a language persists for decades. Taken from Korea as early as three months of age, adult adoptees showed better retention of Korean language and phonology than their Dutch controls during intensive language training. Apparently you can carry a birth language for years after you've left that culture and country.

I hoped this would be true about me. I hoped relearning Korean would be easy. But remembering my mother tongue is difficult.

Excruciatingly and heart-crushingly hard. I spend hours doing home-work, learning sentence structure, new vocabulary, and none of it feels familiar. I feel like I'm in the wilderness. But sometimes, as I struggle to fill in the blanks of my Korean workbook, I hear my mother's voice say the right word in Korean. And I don't feel so lonely.

And then there is Kimberly. Half Korean, half American, like my kids. She has that same hard-to-name quality to her facial features as my children, which sets them apart without quite knowing why. Is it the wide-spaced eyes, the lack of epicanthal folds, the high curve of their cheeks? The hint of something seemingly "exotic," belying the American nature of their gestures and their walk—elongated and carefree, not cautious or restrained. Kimberly displays none of the reservations of a Korean daughter, even though her mother is Korean.

She speaks like any American teenager. "My mother drives me crazy! She bugs me that I eat such unhealthy foods. And then she starts crying that she can't cook for me. 'Ma,' I tell her, 'Stop it! I'm eighteen. Leave me alone!'"

"Kimberly, she's only worried about you."

"I know." She sounds contrite. "She misses me. And I miss her. We're like friends because it's just my mom and me most of the time. I guess we get along so well that it's only the small stuff, like junk food, we argue about. We're actually quite pathetic!" She laughs.

After class one day, Kimberly stands up and turns to me. She is grinning. "I finally had no trouble understanding today's lesson. When I was little and bad, my mother used to say to me a lot, *'Don't do that! Don't touch that!'*"

I laugh. "You didn't understand the previous eleven chapters, but you have grammar pattern 12.2 down. Excellent."

I envy Kimberly's relationship with her mother.

Both my children attend Korean language school at the Korean church for three years, until we move from Pittsburgh. My daughter eagerly participates in Korean dance, and my son practices tae kwon do. They enjoy their activities more than the language classes, but they go every Saturday. Sometimes, after I drop them off, I stand in the quiet side yard of the church and look up at the brilliant stained glass windows. I can picture my daughter sitting at the long cafeteria table in her basement classroom, doodling on the margins of her notebook instead of paying attention to her teacher. She is probably daydreaming about her Korean fan dance performance and her hanbok costume in rainbow colors. I can almost see my son sitting among his younger classmates at the large wooden table in the attic classroom, tracing the Korean alphabet with his crayons—the blue one is his favorite. Given his placid nature, I don't think he pines for his white tae kwon do uniform and yellow belt or yearns to kick his foot through a wooden board, as he once did during a demonstration.

I hope my children feel some connection to their Korean-ness, some sense of where they come from. But I wonder if they feel more estranged. Their father superficially supports their learning Korean, but he doesn't do any of the work: the hours of sitting with them while they do homework, the repetition of vocabulary. He could participate with an electronic Korean-English dictionary, but he's rarely present on Friday nights, excusing himself to his study or the living room when he is actually home. I'm sure it isn't easy for my kids to see so many Korean families, where both the mother and father look the same and the children look unmistakably Korean. I wonder if they feel jealous. My kids never ask me why they look different from me. Maybe because if you get past the fact that they are half Korean, they do look like me. They come home from Korean school with stories about their teachers and classmates, like Koreans are—as Erin puts it—"a fascinating species."

"My Korean dance teacher is amazing," she says. "I don't know how she does it."

"You mean, teach all those children for an hour without a break?"

"Yeah, that too. But what I mean is the way she makes an entrance—several bags of dance costumes hanging off her arms, talking on the phone with her cell phone tucked between her ear and her shoulder, and her three-year-old son crying about something, and her students talking to her at the same time. All she does is hold up her forefinger and say, *Just a minute.'* Like it's no big deal."

"No yelling?" I ask.

"It's chaos all around her and she's totally calm."

"Not like me, you're saying?"

"Nope," she says. "You'd be screaming your head off."

"Thanks."

"You're welcome," she says, without a hint of irony.

My son isn't as impressed by Koreans as his sister. One day he comes home from Korean school and vehemently says he isn't going back, behavior totally unlike him. I ask why.

He sighs deeply. "The Korean girls are too much."

"What do you mean?"

"One girl keeps asking me to sharpen her pencil every time I get up to use the sharpener."

"Liam, you're taller than her. Maybe she can't reach."

"I hate that I'm taller than my classmates."

"You're six. They're still four," I remind him.

"Another girl always wants to sit next to me. She cries if the teacher moves her. Korean girls are so annoying."

I can't help but laugh. "Liam, those girls have a crush on you. It's because you're cute."

He sighs again, looks dejected. "Please, don't make me go to Korean school."

"I'm sorry, honey, but it's good for you. Someday, you're going to thank me."

I am so grateful that this small Korean community has welcomed us, despite the fact that we do not worship at this church. Whenever she sees us, Mrs. Lee always breaks into a huge smile, and she greets my children and me with unflagging enthusiasm.

Sometimes I imagine that I belong here.

When I'm awarded a scholarship to study Korean language at Konkuk University, I find the courage to write a letter to my mother, asking if she could give me the contact information for her sister in Korea. I receive no reply. Reluctantly, I call my sister Susan. My relationship with my sisters is fractured. After our mother was committed to the Carrier Clinic, Sophia and Clara wanted to support her in her own apartment after her release; Susan and I advocated for a psychiatric nursing home. In the quarreling that ensued among the sisters, I was called "a selfish fucking bitch" by more than one of them. Susan capitulated to the other two's demands. Our mother went back into isolation, refusing to answer her door again, and my sisters hated the fact that I was proven right.

When I call my sister Susan and ask if any of the blue aerograms from our mother's old house have our aunt's address, she reads it to me over the phone. I take weeks to compose just a few sentences to my aunt in Korean: *"I hope you remember me. I am Heeseon, the third daughter of your older sister. I will be at Konkuk University for ten weeks this summer and I would love to see you."*

Chapter 14
Parallel Universe

I am standing in an ice-cold mountain stream in Muju, Korea, on a hot summer afternoon in August 2006. The scorching sun cannot combat the goose bumps on my legs. Whenever I lift my feet out of the water and rest them against the back of the opposite leg, my toes feel like icicles. The chill is refreshing, but I flinch from the shock.

I watch my ten-year-old daughter and six-year-old son play with their second cousins. They plunge into the cold water and come up immediately, sputtering but smiling. They climb over huge rock formations to crouch under miniature waterfalls, shivering, as water cascades down the side of this vertiginous mountain into a final torrent that forms this rock pool. Grays and charcoals against a backdrop of lush green. My children look for me and vigorously wave, as if they are checking to make sure I am still here. I smile and lift my hand in a gesture of reassurance. My daughter's blue surf shirt with white hibiscus flowers blends into her brother's solid blue one as they huddle together, their faces obscured by a wall of water. For a moment they are in repose instead of chasing their cousins, splashing and laughing with wanton abandon.

We have come to Muju with Emo, my mother's sister, and her son, my first cousin Joonseuk, and his family. Another first cousin, Daeshik, the son of my mother's brother, and his wife and two children have also joined us on this holiday. My aunt has rented a condo in this popular winter skiing resort to accommodate all six adults and six children. Carrying a modest picnic lunch, we have hiked down a steep path to reach these waterfalls, passing other Koreans far more ambitious with their provisions—portable charcoal grills and still-warm rice in rice cookers, raw bulgogi beef in large plastic containers, lush peaches in baskets.

Daeshik smiles as he watches the young cousins. *"They're having a great time, aren't they?"* he says in Korean.

"They play together like they have known one another forever," Joonseuk says, marveling at the ability of children to adapt to any circumstance.

I want to say that I wish Erin and Liam had known his and Daeshik's children all their lives. Instead, I nod. I voice none of my yearnings.

"Your children don't speak Korean and our children don't speak English well, but they still manage to understand each other and have fun. Nothing stops them," Daeshik says with amusement.

Joonseuk, Daeshik, and I stand side by side in the frigid water, under a cloudless sky. Watching our children. Just passing time. If I close my eyes, I can imagine a parallel universe. I can pretend we have known each other all our lives.

Daeshik, the father of three-year-old Jaewon and five-year-old Minjee, is an affable, self-effacing man, deeply rooted in the Confucian traditions of respect and obedience. He calls me Noona, or "older sister," as Korean culture demands, even though he met me only a week before. He wasn't born when I left Korea, and I have just returned to the country of my birth for the first time at the age of forty-one.

Joonseuk, younger than me by five years, is not so formal. He calls me by my American name. And he speaks in English to me frequently, changing from Korean whenever I have difficulty understanding his more complex sentences and ideas. Joonseuk did some graduate study in America and is facile in English—my brilliant cousin has his PhD in electrical engineering and works for Samsung. Daeshik understands

English but speaks to me only in Korean, and in the more deferential form of speech, rather than the familiar or colloquial.

Korea is a hierarchical society structured around the relationship of a monarch to his subject. Its language reflects its Confucian culture and values. There are six different ways to say something in Korean. The form you choose depends on whether you are speaking to the president or your grandmother or your boss or your parent or a stranger or your friend or your child. These honorific forms strictly adhere to a tiered system of respect. And this hierarchy even exists in the specific words Koreans use, not just in the sentence structure. There are two different words for "sleep" in Korean. The word you use depends on whether you are wishing your grandmother good night or your child good night. And "sleep" is far from the only exception.

Daeshik doesn't call Joonseuk by his given name, even though he has known Joonseuk all his life. Joonseuk is older than Daeshik, who uses the respectful term *hyung*, or "older brother," with his cousin, although they're separated by only two years. I'm older than Daeshik by almost seven years, so I don't think he can even conceive of calling me by my given name.

I find Daeshik's traditional Korean ways endearing. I wish I had been around to hear him call me Noona as he was growing up. He tries to correct me whenever I speak Korean to him in the formal honorific conjugation, repeatedly reminding me to use *ban mal*, which literally translates to "half talk" but means an informal way of speaking. It's how Koreans talk to their children or younger siblings, not older relatives or strangers. Daeshik is pained by the fact that he is younger than me but I address him as though he is older, showing a respect he feels he does not deserve. I tell him it is the only form I am comfortable with when speaking in Korean. He winces but forbears.

Forbearance is a hallmark trait of Koreans. Korea is *"the shrimp between two whales."* The culture and people have survived for more than five thousand years between two countries intent on conquest—a behemoth China and a war-driven Japan. Koreans have had to possess an enduring patience and forbearance.

∽

When Daeshik was driving me from the Gwangju tree farm where our grandmother lives to Muju to meet Joonseuk for this sojourn, we talked as my children slept in the back seat of his car. He told me that his father and Joonseuk's mother were the two closest siblings of our grandmother's five children. While growing up, he spent many holidays with Joonseuk.

"I wish I had grown up in Korea," I said.

"I think we would have had a great time," Daeshik agreed.

"I would have teased you and made you do things for me." I smiled at him.

He glanced away from the road and smiled back. *"Noona, of course, that is a given."*

"Did you always listen to Joonseuk?" I teased.

Daeshik's face became serious. *"Hyung was a good oldest sibling. He looked out for the rest of us. He was kind and good. He still is."*

I shook my head. *"Maybe Emo is right, I am not Korean. I don't understand this business of being the oldest. I think Joonseuk is burdened by being the oldest cousin."*

"The oldest has responsibilities the younger ones do not have, especially the oldest son," said Daeshik.

"My father was the jangsohn. My mother hated my grandfather. He blamed her for not having any sons. We moved to Uganda." I thought about my mother, who traversed oceans and entire continents to get away from her father-in-law and the fact that her husband was the last jangsohn. Yet she could not escape her self-imposed shame. I knew Daeshik's mother had also married the oldest son, my uncle. I turned to him. *"What was it like for your mother?"*

"My mother had to live with our grandmother. Our grandmother was not a kind woman. I saw how brutally she treated my mother," said Daeshik.

"And that didn't make you angry?" I switched to English in my surprise.

"At the time, it did. But our grandmother is an old woman now. She has lost her husband. She is losing her mind." Daeshik's voice was calm.

"You have no anger toward her?" I said, probing beneath the surface.

"What would be the point? She is an old woman," he said, no trace of resentment in his tone.

"So you forgive her? After what she has done to your mother?" I was still skeptical.

"We are Korean. We must forbear."

What Daeshik said reminded me of a conversation Joonseuk and I had when we went to Seoraksan, one of the most beautiful mountains in Korea. Joonseuk's wife had put their two children to bed and gone to sleep herself. Joonseuk and I sat drinking beer at the kitchen table of the condo they'd rented for that weekend trip of hiking trails and playing in water parks.

"Are you happy as a writer?" he had asked.

"Much happier than when I was a doctor," I answered.

"I think I could have been an artist," Joonseuk said.

"Don't you like being an engineer?" I asked in English, surprised.

"My father was an electrical engineer, so there was pressure for me to be the same. I didn't resist. But now I wish I had done something different. I think you are brave for leaving medicine and becoming a writer."

"Brave or stupid. I can't decide which," I said. "What would you have done if you could do it again?"

"Maybe a violinist?" he suggested in English.

"I didn't know you played the violin." I was taken aback by his revelation.

"When I was young, I liked playing the violin but I gave it up. Maybe I could have been really good."

"And you could have been a concert violinist?" I smiled.

He laughed. *"Maybe. I'm not sure I want to be an engineer anymore."*

"There's always time to do something else if you want," I urged.

Joonseuk looked pensive. *"It is too late. I have a wife and two children. I have responsibilities."*

I sighed. "Joonseuk, I think sometimes you are too responsible."

"I am the oldest sibling to my sisters, and all of our cousins. I have to set a good example."

"I'm sorry my sisters and I left Korea and stuck you with this terrible job."

"Many times I wished you had not left Korea. I'm glad you have come back. It has been very comforting to have an older sister around."

"I wish you had been my actual younger sibling. I think we would have gotten along well. Not like my sisters and me."

"Why is the relationship so difficult between you and your sisters?"

I didn't tell Joonseuk that there were so many resentments my sisters harbored toward me. The fact that I was taller than them. That they felt I was smarter, and a show-off. That it was an unfair competition my mother forced upon them, when I was clearly her favorite. That I became the doctor in the family and then abandoned it all. When I told my sisters I was leaving the practice of medicine, one sister said with outrage, "You can't stop being a doctor. That's not something people do!" Another sister said, "Of course, you decide one day that you want to be a writer, and it happens. Life isn't as easy for the rest of us."

I didn't know how to tell Joonseuk all this, in Korean or in English for that matter, so I responded with a quip. "They're mad at me because I'm taller than they are."

"And you are the prettiest?" he teased.

I laughed. "Of course!"

Koreans have a saying: *"In a house rich with daughters, the third is the most beautiful."* In olden times, during the height of arranged marriages, a wedding could be brokered between a man and a woman, sight unseen, if she was the third daughter, because of the prevalence of this belief by Koreans.

Once, when all my sisters and I were gathered around the swimming pool of my sister Sophia's country club, a Korean friend of hers said this upon meeting us: "It's true what Koreans say about the third daughter being the most beautiful."

My sister Clara was irate in her response: "I completely disagree!"

My sister Sophia nodded with resignation.

My sister Susan just shrugged.

I laughed and pretended her comment was a joke.

"I suspect you are the most accomplished and articulate of your sisters. It is not your fault." Joonseuk looked at me. His eyes had a depth of kindness that I have never seen from my own siblings.

"Now I really wish we had grown up together." My eyes prickled with impending tears. I took a sip of beer to stop myself from crying.

After we return to the condo from our afternoon at the mountain stream, we scatter. My cousins and I agree to meet for dinner with our families at one of the many restaurants in the resort complex. My mother's sister is going back to her home in Daejun with her husband. She says she's had enough excitement and she's letting the young people enjoy themselves. I walk her down to the parking lot, my arm linked with hers. I will miss her when I return to America. For the past two months, she has called me in Seoul every Sunday morning to ask how I'm doing. I am already nostalgic for those phone calls, even as I know that she will call me tomorrow, before my departure.

"I want to tell you something," Emo says.

We are standing next to her car. Her husband has stowed the luggage and is waiting in the driver's seat.

She takes both of my hands in hers. *"I am so happy you came to Korea. I have wanted to see you for so long."*

I smile, but a part of me wants to cry. *"I'm glad I came. I'm sorry to give you the news about my mother."* I give Emo a hug. *"I hope she will get better soon and both of us will come back to visit you in Korea."* I say this with an optimism I do not feel.

I remember the first time I saw my beautiful aunt after returning to Korea. After receiving my letter asking to see her while I was studying at Konkuk University for the summer, she called the front desk of the International Guest House, where I was staying, and came looking for me. I remember walking down the ramp of the oddly shaped, circular language-learning building on Konkuk's campus to find my aunt at the bottom. Even in the sea of Korean faces, I recognized her immediately—her face a diminutive, softer version of my mother's. She and her husband took me on a tour of Seoul that lasted well into the night.

At one point during that day, we wandered through the grounds of Deoksugung, a summer palace of the Joseon dynasty emperors. On a dusty path under a blazing-blue sky, my aunt abruptly stopped walking and gripped my arm. Earlier in the day, she had asked me how my mother was doing. I told her that my mother had been very sick but was no longer in the hospital. I wanted to say more but didn't know how, and my aunt had not pursued the matter.

"What happened isn't your fault. How your mother chose to live her life has nothing to do with you or your sisters," Emo said, her voice low and urgent.

We were alone, standing under the shade of a royal tile roof that was bluish appearing from the angle of the descending sun.

"Your mother was willful and spoiled. She was our mother's favorite. Whenever I argued with my sister, our mother always made me apologize, no matter whose fault it was." Emo sighed with regret.

I did not know that my mother had been the favorite child. And I had not considered the burden of expectation that she carried, even as she enjoyed the benefits of that role.

My aunt and I continued the conversation at her home in Daejun. She was cooking a Korean feast of bulgogi, jhap chae, and so many other dishes, just for me. She and Joonseuk's wife had been stuck in the kitchen for most of the day. While she chopped vegetables, I finally told her about my mother's suicide attempt. Even while cutting onions, she did not cry. But later that evening, after dinner, we watched a Korean drama in which the woman protagonist loses her lover and is heartbroken. My aunt started crying and could not seem to stop.

In Muju, Emo says, *"I hope you will come back to see me soon."*

"Don't worry, you can't get rid of me so easily." I try to be flippant.

There is so much kindness in Emo's eyes as she looks at me. She is wise and compassionate with her advice. *"Live a good life. Don't let the tragedy of your mother's life ruin yours. You deserve a good life."*

After my aunt's car has disappeared from view, I lean back against the red wood siding of the building and allow the tears to fall down my cheeks. I don't try to stop them. I take deep breaths and wait for them to subside. Then I step back inside and head for the stairs up to the condo. In the lobby, I see Daeshik's son standing in front of a vending machine, seemingly mesmerized.

"Jaewon, what are you doing?"

Only minutes before, all the second cousins had been together in the living room, watching the animated movie *Cars.*

His miniature form, the top of his head barely reaching my thighs, turns to face me. *"I want juice. Can I have it?"*

"I'm not sure. Where's your father?" I look around for my cousin.

"Upstairs." Jaewon stares at the tiny can with a picture of a peach, his hand tapping the glass. *"Can I have the juice?"*

"I think we should ask your father first," I answer, although I'm pretty sure my cousin won't have a problem with his son having peach juice.

He pulls himself up to full height, throws his head back, and shouts for his father, *"Ah-paa!"*

"Jaewon, he can't hear you."

"Ah-paa!" he yells louder.

I put my hands over my ears. *"Okay, okay, you can have the juice."* Jaewon smiles at me.

My cousins and I go out to dinner with our families, and we fight over who gets to pay. Koreans take it as a point of honor to pay the bill, especially when they consider themselves the hosts in the situation. I finally win for the first time this weekend, but I cheat. I take the waitress aside and give her money in advance. Joonseuk and Daeshik both shake their heads at me and say that I should not pay. I tell them that I am not their guest but their *noona,* their older sister, so I should have paid the whole weekend.

After dinner we meander through the various souvenir shops and boutiques in the resort. Daeshik's wife buys stuffed animals for my children—a Scottie dog for my daughter and a brown bear for my son—despite my objection that they are too old for such things. My children are happy that I have been vetoed. We walk in the warm night air toward multicolored lights and the sounds of a carnival. Our children run ahead, begging for sweets. We buy them cotton candy. We wait for them to be finished with their Ferris wheel rides. Daeshik's wife says that it's getting late and the children are tired. We take one last picture. Joonseuk, Daeshik, and I stand next to one another, surrounded by our children, and laugh into the camera.

We are saying our goodbyes when five-year-old Minjee bursts into tears. It's almost eleven o'clock at night, and I assume she is overwrought. First her mother tries to hold her, but she sinks to the ground, inconsolable. Daeshik crouches down, puts his head next to hers. I cannot hear him clearly, but I can tell he's asking his daughter questions, and when she responds, he sounds like he's scolding her. He picks her up, holds her to his chest, and speaks softly. *"It is going to be all right. You are going to be fine."* She cries even harder. I walk over to where he is gently rocking his daughter, patting her back.

"Is something wrong? Can I do anything to help?" I ask.

"Nothing is wrong." He waves away my concern.

"I am a pediatrician, not just a writer," I offer.

"Minjee is being silly," he says.

"She must be tired," I suggest.

Daeshik smiles at me. *"Minjee is upset because she doesn't want Liam to go home. She says she is in love with your son and she wants to marry him. She is crying because she doesn't want him to go back to America."*

I can't help myself. I laugh. *"Does she know that a five-year-old and a six-year-old can't get married yet?"*

Daeshik pretends to be chagrined. *"I told her that cousins cannot marry. That only upset her more. She says she loves Liam and they must get married."*

"She is already so sure of her love? After only a few days? Maybe she should wait a little while longer."

Daeshik shakes his head. *"She says she is absolutely certain. They are going to get married."*

In a parallel universe, Daeshik, Joonseuk, and I stand side by side in the same ice-cold mountain stream in Muju and talk about our children. We go out to dinner. Our children ride the same carnival rides. We take the same picture together with our families. Minjee still wants to marry Liam. Daeshik drives me back to Seoul late at night.

But I don't leave the next morning to go back to America.

Instead, I live in Seoul, in a neighborhood close to my cousins. My children go to school with their second cousins. I visit my mother in Gwangju on weekends. She is happy; she is not in a psychiatric hospital.

She scolds me to come visit more often with my children. Sometimes I go to Seoraksan with Joonseuk and hike a trail with stunning vistas of waterfalls and timberline. We talk about our careers as a writer and a violinist. We stop and stare at the face of Buddha carved into the mountainside. We drive back in the stream of weekend traffic on a Sunday night, with all the other Koreans returning to Seoul.

Chapter 15
Blue Petals on the Wall

His initials are SS. Another red flag I will be reminded of by a therapist many years later that I ignored. We met during medical school. I was on the rebound from my first love affair—something that should have happened to me in high school or college. SS was not tall, not good-looking, which was actually in his favor since I wanted nothing to do with a handsome man. He seemed nice and funny—he told me he had been the class clown in high school.

I didn't agonize over whether or not he loved me. I didn't want to go through another emotionally fraught relationship like the one I'd had with my ex-boyfriend: years of breaking up and getting back together again and again. When SS said, "I love you," I felt relief. And I responded, "I love you too."

Because one day, post call, feeling grungy and beyond tired, I had come home to a clean apartment. When I thanked him, he said, "I want to spend my life taking care of you. I love you." I thought I had found my Prince Charming. Never mind that he did not clean my apartment ever again.

I thought I would be safe, not only from the agonies of true love, but from the infidelity of Korean men. SS never met my parents because he was not Korean, a characteristic my mother in particular would look at with strong disapproval, and because I was not supposed to be dating, even though I was twenty-six years old.

Then I became pregnant. In my last year of medical school, I had already committed to a pediatric residency in another city. I turned to SS for support and guidance because I could not go to my conservative Korean parents. My mother had instructed me that I had to be a virgin on my wedding night. Clean and untouched. I couldn't imagine the depths of her rage if she found out that I was not only unclean but pregnant too. I already felt promiscuous for having had sex with two men in my life: my ex-boyfriend and SS. How could I possibly tell my mother that I had sex before marriage? And I could not fathom even having a conversation about pregnancy with my father.

SS said, "I love you and want to marry you. But a baby is not what we need." He sounded logical, reasonable. "You would have to quit residency. Do you want to give up everything you've worked for?" he said. Not once did he talk about the possibility of him giving up his medical residency to stay home with our child.

I pictured my mother at the crossroad, pregnant with my oldest sister. The moment when she chose to believe my father and his claims of fidelity. I didn't want a baby. I had so much student loan debt that I felt like I had no choice but to get on with my medical career. How else was I going to pay back that money? But the thought of an abortion made me want to throw up, cry uncontrollably.

"I'm only thinking about what's best for you," SS said during one of our gut-wrenching talks about abortion. "We must marry in the Catholic Church because it's important to my mother and to me. A baby will ruin everything. I just want what's best for you." He said those words with such sincerity, his voice earnest, his face a study in contemplation.

I had an abortion. And I clung to him like a lifeline: I was supposed to be with SS; he was the father of my child. On June 25, 1994, I stood in a Catholic church in a white dress, holding his hand, and vowed to love and honor him and forsake all others.

~⁓

The first time SS threw a dish we were living together, not yet married. I was sitting at our rickety table for two, the metal feet at the bottom of the wood stand barely able to support its weight. I can't remember what we were arguing about. It was probably something trivial. I was crying and he was saying, "You're mistaken. You don't know what you're saying," his voice calm.

He had generously cooked dinner that night: frozen chicken fingers thawed in a toaster oven along with Tater Tots, all served with ketchup. I was post call from working thirty-six-plus hours at the hospital, but he was not, so he offered to wash the dishes as well. I had showered before dinner; my shoulder-length black hair was wet. Wisps of my damp hair brushed against my cheek as the dish whizzed past me and shattered on the wall. Red globs of ketchup splattered on my neck.

This is not happening. I am in a nightmare. I will wake up. When confronted with sudden violence, my reaction was always one of denial. Foolish hope that whatever was happening would magically disappear. Then I could pretend it never happened.

"What is wrong with you?" he screamed, his face crimson, his hands pounding the rim of the metal sink.

I sat motionless, willing my body to grow smaller and smaller. *Invisible.*

"Why do you have to be this way?" His rage flared and consumed all the oxygen in the room.

I kept my head down, my eyes tracking him under lowered lids.

He ran to the kitchen door, flung it open, and stomped onto the brick patio. He snatched a terracotta pot off the ground, arced it over his head, and smashed it. He did it again and again. The clattering and screeching of ceramic shards bouncing off red brick echoed into the night.

It's my fault. I asked him to forgive me.

"Please don't make me lose my temper again," he said, his voice quiet and heavy with disappointment.

I still remember the pattern of blue flowers on the wallpaper of that kitchen. The half-open flowers seemed cheery, the leafy green stems curving and spiraling up to the blank white ceiling. A part of me is still sitting at that rickety table, staring at the lavender-blue petals on the wall.

∽

My throat burned. But I was in denial. My head didn't ache; my muscles weren't sore; I didn't have a fever. Just the feeling someone was cauterizing the back of my mouth with a torch whenever I swallowed. But on the plane, I felt alternately hot and freezing cold. By the time I got off the AirTrain at JFK, I was dragging my red suitcase so slowly that everyone was passing me by. I got on the E train to Penn Station; I didn't even think of taking a cab. I stared at the giant train board at Penn Station—the next New Jersey Transit train to Newark was forty minutes away, and then I would still have to take another train to the suburb where we lived.

I called SS.

In the fall of 2008, we'd gone to New Orleans for a long weekend because he was being paid by a pharmaceutical company to attend a "symposium": code for a little bit of medical education and a lot of eating meals at expensive restaurants like Emeril's so the company could thank their most prolific lecturers and prescribers of drugs. All of his expenses were covered. All we had to do was pay for my airfare. So I found the cheapest ticket, one that required me to go to JFK on the return, not Newark, the airport near our home in New Jersey. It was a hundred dollars cheaper. SS applauded my frugality, even though he knew I would have to spend more than two hours getting home from JFK to New Jersey by public transit. He was going direct to Newark Airport and then taking a car service twenty minutes home.

SS didn't answer his cell phone or the house phone. I pictured him under the rain head of the glass shower enclosure in our slate-and-marble bathroom and longed for steam to unclog the congestion and pressure building in my head. I got on a NJ Transit train to Newark. By the time I hit the large echo of the center of the station, my body was coated with sweat from a raging fever. I bought chamomile tea drenched with three packets of sugar—glucose to keep me going.

I called SS.

When he answered the phone, I could barely speak, my voice just above a whisper.

"I can't hear you," he said.

I repeated myself.

"Are you sure you can't take the train home? I just got back from a run, and I need to cool down before I take a shower."

I pleaded.

"Why don't you drink your tea? You'll feel better and then you can take the train home."

He hung up. I drank my tea. I got up and started dragging my suitcase to the ticket machines. I became dizzy and sat back down.

I called SS.

Instead of his previous cajoling tone, his voice had an edge: "I'm cooling down. And I still have to get in a shower. And then it's going to take me another twenty minutes to get there. It would be easier if I just picked you up at the train station here."

I cried.

"Fine, I'm coming. But you're going to have to wait."

He didn't show up for almost an hour. I apologized when I got into the passenger seat. He sighed; he wouldn't look at me. I broke down, my body shaking with sobs. The tea in a paper cup jostled in my left hand from the vibration of my body quivering. The now-tepid liquid escaped from the drinking spout of the lid and spilled onto the center console of his Mercedes, and a few drops fell onto my leather seat.

"Oh no, I'm sorry," I whispered. I leaned forward, opening the glove compartment, looking for napkins to wipe up the drops.

"Look at what you've done!" he screamed.

He threw his clenched fist at me. I jerked away, protecting my face. His fist landed on my shoulder, arms, and rib cage, his arm hinging and unhinging at the elbow again and again. Like a hammer. Knocked out of my hand, the paper teacup landed on the floor, soaking the carpet. I covered my head with my arms, hunched against the window, pressing my body as far away from him as possible. He screamed about how he was always sacrificing for me and our children, how he did everything for us and never for himself, his voice screeching and reverberating in the stale air of the enclosed car.

This isn't happening. I am in a nightmare. I will wake up.

I told myself those things even though, for years, he had rages in which he screamed until his face turned purple. When he threw anything within reach—a cup of mismatched pens and pencils raining like missiles, a leather belt that snaked like a whip, drinking goblets that became glass shards. When he would imprint on my arms smudges of black and blue that turned yellow and green. When I would run up the stairs and lock myself in the bathroom while he pounded on the door.

And I stayed silent. Because he always apologized after his heinous acts. Because he seemed so contrite that he had hurt me. He did this so I would stay. And then he behaved as though these incidents had never happened.

Ironic, but he was the one who left in 2011 because he was dallying with several women. I don't think I could ever have left. I was too damaged, too dangerously invested in the narrative that we were a happy family: husband, wife, and two children. I'd spent years as a physician staying quiet when I was sexually harassed because I was surrounded by men. I was used to being beaten down. And SS convinced me that I was the problem. I was "antisocial"; I was "depressed"; I had "no friends." My mother had tried to kill herself and my immigrant family was dysfunctional. I was more than ready to take blame—I thought if it was my fault, then I could fix it. A therapist once pointed out that I, being a masochist who constantly blamed myself for the failure of my marriage, and who stayed in it for twenty years, was perfect prey for what the therapist casually called "a charming narcissist" like SS.

I thought it was my fault that SS asked for a divorce while I was in Korea in the summer of 2006, because I'd left him to parent our children alone for six weeks before they all joined me; it was my fault that we lost a hundred thousand dollars when we sold our house and moved after only a year because our children, especially our daughter, were being bullied at school. It was my fault that I didn't know she wanted to kill herself because of the bullying, and when she finally confided in me and I told him, his response was, "How could you keep this from me?"—despite the fact that the year before, I had said that I had suspected as much. And all he did was continuously complain about how much money we had lost.

In attempting to reframe my way of thinking, the therapist also pointed out that in being a masochist, I was being arrogant: I thought if I took all the blame, then I could also fix everything. I thought I had more power than I really did. But I think believing in that misguided logic was my only option, because I could not acknowledge the horrific mistake I had made in marrying SS. That would mean admitting to failure. Now it astounds me what I was willing to do not to admit failure.

SS spent hundreds of thousands of dollars on lawyers so he wouldn't have to pay child support. He spent more money on legal fees than he would ever pay in the financial support of our children. At first he tried to say that he loved them very much but couldn't "afford" to pay. Then he got remarried and had two more children. Then he stopped pretending he was poor. But it didn't make up for the fact that I went to court—supreme court, family court, bankruptcy court, appellate court—forty-four times over eight years, with fifteen justices, judges, support magistrates, and custody referees involved in those court battles.

I wish I could say that I transcended those experiences. I did not. I wish I could say that I did it smiling and with grace and aplomb. Nope. I wept in frustration until I was hiccupping. I hated every second of it. I hated every sleepless night before a court date, the bile rising in my throat, the feeling that I was suffocating, that my heart would beat right out of my chest because I was so terrified. I hated every judge who refused to see what SS was doing to our children and refused to find him in contempt, even though it was the fourth time—not counting the seven previous sessions during our divorce trial—we were appearing in front of her because he refused to pay his court-ordered obligations.

Yes, Justice Barbara Jaffe, I'm talking about you.

And I hated feeling so helpless. So afraid.

Then our daughter dropped out of college over Thanksgiving 2014, only months after she started. I was the only parent who had gone on college tours with her, labored over the Common Application and all its intricacies with her, held her hand as she clicked open admissions decisions from eight different colleges. And only a few weeks after she withdrew, SS proposed a deal in which I would give up claim to forty-eight thousand dollars, and in return he would not file for yet another downward modification of child support and would drop his appeal of the judgment of divorce in appellate court. It was unlikely he would have been successful in either attempt, but I didn't negotiate. I agreed to his terms. I thought if I gave him what he wanted, he would stop his relentless bullying.

I was wrong. After I agreed to his proposed deal, he came back and said that he also wanted me to take child support payments out of the purview of the Support Collection Unit, a government organization that collects and distributes child support payments. It had taken me three years to get the Office of Child Support Enforcement to garnish his wages. Three years of no payment or partial payments. I said absolutely not. *When hell freezes over.* I had agreed to all his conditions. But he wanted more. And when I wouldn't give him more, he walked away from his own deal.

That was when I knew.

SS was never going to stop. It wasn't about money. It was about control—imposing his will, imposing his narrative. And I had better learn how to combat him. I wish I could say that I stood up and put my hands on my hips and said, "Bring it on," with assurance and confidence. Nope. I dreaded whatever petty, vindictive thing SS would do next. I dreaded the churning of my stomach, the need to close my eyes and force myself to exhale. To keep breathing. But a mantra sprang up in my head: *I refuse to live in fear.* I had to keep saying it over and over and over again before I was able to believe one word. Before I thought it was even possible.

In October 2016, SS filed a writ of habeas corpus in Family Court of the State of New York, claiming I kidnapped our son because we moved to Oregon. Instead of being grateful that he didn't have to pay private school tuition any longer, SS went after custody of our son. Even though their relationship had frayed to the point that our son had not seen him for the previous three years, SS wanted to maintain his facade of loving father, regardless of his actions to the contrary. And despite our son calling and begging him to withdraw the writ, he refused.

I wasn't a lawyer. I didn't know what I was doing. But I didn't have the money to pay a lawyer anymore, so I appeared in court by myself. I represented myself through the countless times SS dragged me back to court to stop his child support payments and gain custody of our son.

I learned to write ninety-seven-page legal documents in opposition to SS, with help from a pro-bono lawyer who worked for a nonprofit that helps women survive domestic violence. And I started watching Korean dramas again. I didn't know why at first. I just knew that for sixteen episodes I could be someone else: a blind Korean heiress who finds true love; a poor Korean girl who marries an arrogant rich man against her will but ends up falling in love with him; a girl who pretends to be a boy to get a job at a coffee shop, only to fall in love with the male owner, who also falls in love with her, even though he thinks she is a boy. I needed those alternate stories because SS was trying to destroy me. I needed to cling to a story of me that could have been possible if I had not left Seoul.

And I did not remain silent.

I don't mean to imply that it was easy. Every cell, every sinew of my body braced for impact each time I spoke up for myself. I felt like vomiting. And my voice was shaking. But I opposed his attorney's argument to stop child support payments when SS went back to family court again, after he didn't get the result he wanted in the Supreme Court of the State of New York. And the support magistrate had to uphold the law. As much as it aggrieved her, because she didn't like me: "You don't know when to keep quiet!"

⁓

I like to imagine that a part of me is still sitting at that rickety table, staring at the blue flowers on the wallpaper of that kitchen in that house where SS and I lived before we married. I think about the possibility that I could have gotten up from that table, walked down the hallway to our bedroom, packed a suitcase of my things, and left that night. That possibility makes me believe in a parallel universe where it actually happened. That I got away from him.

And I like to imagine that a part of my mother is still standing at the crossroad all those years ago, when she was pregnant with my oldest sister. I like to imagine that my father was in the middle of telling his lies when the bus pulls up. I picture my mother saying that she won't go back to him, that she deserves better. I want to believe that my mother gets on that bus and doesn't look back.

"We tell ourselves stories in order to live," said Joan Didion. A friend once told me that she was trying to turn "the flaming wreckage" of her life into a story. Perhaps everyone has a flaming wreckage of a life. We can choose to watch it burn. Or we can take the jagged pieces and make a new life with the repaired seams evident, stark and startling and beautiful. The story of my life doesn't have to be either that I made a catastrophic mistake in marrying a narcissistic sociopath *or* that I lived happily ever after. It can be that I made a catastrophic mistake in marrying a narcissistic sociopath *and* I still lived happily ever after.

It is possible.

Chapter 16
Bagpipes Play in Central Park

I was on Park Loop Road heading to the Harlem Meer when I heard the bagpipes. I was so startled I stopped walking. A cyclist whizzed past me. *Maybe I'm hearing things,* I thought. But the high-pitched wailing continued. I looked around and saw a couple of women in lululemon walking on the other side of the road, talking animatedly to each other. If they'd heard the sudden burst of bagpipes, surely they would have stopped talking and looked toward the direction of the sound, right? More cyclists passed me. I stifled the urge to ask a couple coming from the other direction, "I know this sounds crazy, but do you hear bagpipes?" My pride wouldn't let me do it.

No self-respecting New Yorker asks a question of another New Yorker. We have an unspoken rule: Thou shalt not disturb thy neighbor. I've been yelled at on a subway platform by another woman: "You dropped it!" By the time I had picked up my wayward MetroCard, she was gone, my "Thank you!" finding no one.

I walked in what I thought was the direction of the bagpipes—which were, by the way, very loud. I descended a steep hill and steered into a part of Central Park where I'd never been. Having walked the park for almost two years now, I was shocked that there was this hidden section not yet revealed to me. Curious, I glanced at tall columns and a wide lawn to my right, and to my left, imposing metal gates and marble steps leading to Fifth Avenue, walking as quickly as I could toward the sound of bagpipes. I didn't want to look silly or possibly even unhinged if I ran in one direction, then stopped dead and ran off again in a different direction, based on the waxing and waning of the music. But if I walked erratically, I'd look perfectly normal. After all, I'd seen so many people do that before—walk rapidly in one direction, only to stop and veer off in another.

By 2013, I had observed eccentric if not frankly bizarre behavior in Central Park. I once caught a man urinating behind a tree, only to apologize to him before running off while he remained unperturbed. Lovers with their clothes half-off during daylight didn't see my embarrassment as I abruptly turned away from them and didn't seem to hear my coughing. These instances were rare, but the woman who ran in her actual bra, not a sports bra, was a consistent fixture around the Central Park Reservoir.

I think that walking in Central Park may have saved my life. In April 2011, SS had just left "the marital abode," as our condo became known during our divorce. I had been staring at my bedroom ceiling in the dark, despairing because I couldn't sleep through another night, when a thought popped into my head: *I can walk in the park. Hardly anyone will be there at four o'clock in the morning, and I can cry without anyone seeing.* Even though our condo in Harlem was four blocks from Park Loop Road, I had only occasionally gone there. But somehow that strange thought in the early-morning hours of that day spurred me out of bed, and I was walking in the park before dawn broke over New York. I did cry that first time I walked, before returning home to get my kids ready for school. But the shame of crying in front of strangers stopped me on subsequent outings. I walked in the park almost every day, sometimes several times a day. My favorite loop was to go up the Great Hill, then descend to the duck pond, cross over to the baseball fields, go up a small hill, pass the tennis courts, to end up at a bridge to the reservoir.

The Jacqueline Kennedy Onassis Reservoir is the single most beautiful thing in Central Park. In my opinion anyway. The path around the reservoir is 1.6 miles, and in my best running days I could cover it twice. I started running during my divorce. Perhaps I was trying to outrun the divorce litigation of my narcissistic sociopath of an ex-husband. Perhaps I was trying to outrun my pain. I know I blamed myself in those early days of the divorce. I told everyone that I had to fix it. SS said that I had become depressed and gained ten pounds and let myself go. I was sure that I was the problem. And when my sisters heard about my divorce, they tried to support me at first. At least I choose to believe that, because I want to believe that difficulty can forge bonds and bring a family together, despite the evidence to the contrary when my mother tried to commit suicide and my sisters and I became estranged. But my sisters' efforts were limited and stunted. One sister took me to a resort in Arizona in late May when temperatures were over a hundred degrees, but said, "He left you because you're so self-absorbed." When I asked how I was being selfish, she said, "All you did was talk about your patients, the kids in the hospital, when you were in residency." At the time, it didn't occur to me to say, "Really? All those sick and dying children?" Another sister invited me to her house in the suburbs, and I gratefully spent several weekends of one summer there. But she said, "When he takes you back, you have to do everything. The cooking, the cleaning, the laundry. Everything." I didn't say that I already did those things. I just nodded. But only six months into my divorce, when I called one sister to ask for a loan of five hundred dollars, she said that she couldn't lend me the money because she was saving for her daughter's college fund. Never mind that she drove a Volvo SUV and paid tens of thousands of dollars to belong to a country club. Another sister, when asked for the five-hundred-dollar loan, said that I had borrowed two hundred dollars from her while I was in medical school and hadn't paid it back, so she couldn't take another chance with me. I finally summoned the indignation to say that she must be mistaken. I was sure I would have paid back a loan taken more than twenty years earlier. And if I hadn't, why hadn't she mentioned it to me sooner? I didn't bother calling the third sister.

Now it was May 2013, and I had just finished running the reservoir after returning from my writing conference in Tempe. While there, I had learned that SS had filed for bankruptcy, even though he would start a new job in July, even though he was still receiving severance from the job he had left in March. Standing in the hundred-degree Arizona heat, I felt cold and numb. I was shaking like I had chills from a fever. I had been on the phone with the bank that held the home equity loan on the condo in which my children and I lived. We had been negotiating new terms for the loan when the bank officer, after putting me on hold, returned and told me that the entire amount of one hundred twenty-eight thousand dollars was now due. Immediately. She said that the primary mortgage was also in default. The bank was going to foreclose on our apartment because of SS's declaration of bankruptcy. Never mind we were divorced. Never mind that *I* hadn't filed for bankruptcy. My children and I were going to lose our home.

In Central Park, I had been blasting Alicia Keys's "Girl on Fire" and Kelly Clarkson's "Stronger" through my earbuds, my ultimate playlist for running the reservoir. It's ironic that "Stronger" is one of my favorite songs. When I was younger and still married to SS, I expressed my ire with the cliché "What doesn't kill you makes you stronger" as meaningless and misleading. I said that terrible things happening to you didn't make you stronger. And SS would say, "Yes, you're right. What doesn't kill you makes you weaker for the next blow. Until you're dead." Now I see that during our divorce, he was relentlessly trying to deliver the next blow. Now I believe that terrible things happening to you shape you, and that you can choose to learn from the experience. Now I believe in resilience.

Sweat still dripping from my face after my run, I took my usual path from the reservoir to the east side of Park Loop Road, on my way to the Harlem Meer. I was inhaling warm spring air and tilting my face to the sun, trying to convert more vitamin D into active form, when I heard the bagpipes playing. I suppose I shouldn't have been startled to hear bagpipes in a park. I had heard them before when I lived in Pittsburgh, a few months after Poppy, my father-in-law, died. It was easy to find the bagpiper in Mellon Park, standing on top of a hill, dressed in khaki pants and a white shirt of all things.

Bagpipes had played at Poppy's funeral in 2004, the same year I left the practice of medicine. He knew I wanted to be a writer, and he was happy for me. We had spoken about it on the phone, he in New Jersey and I in Pittsburgh. I was perched on the staircase of my house. It was night and I could see my reflection in the glass front door, my face wrinkling and ugly-crying. It was a week before his death. He had joined a twelve-step program because his wife insisted he was an alcoholic, although he had never shown signs of delirium tremens or alcohol withdrawal. But after losing his job he had become depressed and secluded himself at their beach house, not showing up for family events or participating in birthday celebrations for about a year. He had called to make amends to those he'd hurt. I acknowledged that he'd hurt me. I said that I had missed him and was happy to have him back. He said that he loved me and that he was proud of me. He said he would try as hard as he could so his grandchildren would be proud of him.

The day before his death, I only gave him a kiss on the cheek before sailing out his kitchen door for the airport. He had volunteered to babysit my children while SS and I were in California for one of SS's medical conferences. I heard about his death on a rainy day in Napa Valley. At one point on the flight back, there was so much turbulence that I thought the plane was going to crash. Gripping the armrests with both hands, I resigned myself to perishing and said over and over in my head, *I love you, Erin. I love you, Liam,* when I suddenly heard whistling.

I looked up to see Poppy strolling down the aisle in a ratty T-shirt and shorts and battered sneakers, his usual getup for fishing. I was too astounded to say anything.

He smiled and said, "You're going to be okay, Pook." He started walking away.

"Wait, Poppy. I don't want you to go," I said.

"I love you, Pook. You're going to be fine," he said, looking back, then continued whistling and walking.

"I love you too, Poppy." My voice caught in my throat, and I squeezed my eyes shut to stop the tears.

When I opened my eyes again, the plane stopped shuddering and pitching. The pilot came on the speaker and assured us passengers that there would be no more turbulence. A freak incident, he said.

I looked around, searching. As though Poppy would still be there.

I called him Poppy, and he called me Pook. Only now do I appreciate the alliterative nature of our nicknames. I had avoided calling him anything while I was engaged to be married to his son. "Dad" was too close to what I called my father, and using his first name seemed too informal, not respectful enough. After all, I was Korean. One morning at his house—I'm not sure if I was married or still engaged—he bought bagels and brought them into the kitchen. I was standing by the round glass-top table and asked him why poppy seed was his favorite. I'm not sure what his answer was. But I remember my response: "I should call you Poppy Seed!" He smiled and said, "Let's keep it simple. Poppy." The name stuck.

He wasn't a television person, but he found the sitcom *Murphy Brown*, with its sly humor, worth watching. He thought Candice Bergen, playing a news anchor, was sharp and beautiful and her young producer on the show, Miles, was an endearing goofball. When Miles finally found a girlfriend and they started using the endearment Pookie, Poppy found it hilarious. He said to SS and me, "You should call each other that." I groaned and threatened to throw a pillow at him. He laughed. "Come on, Pookie, it's funny." Eventually he shortened it to Pook. The name stuck.

He loved me like a daughter, without all the baggage of actually being blood related. He paid off my student loans before he paid off his son's. He said it was because mine had higher interest rates, and he was sensible like that, but I think it was because he liked me. Clearly SS carried resentment, listing his student loans as joint debt and his father's payment of my loans ten years prior as assets to which he felt entitled during our divorce. SS was a narcissist like my father, only thinking of how things affected him, not anyone else. He was not like Poppy.

Poppy loved Christmas, and even after his kids had entered their thirties, he staged extravagant gift openings on Christmas mornings. Among my many presents one year was a dozen golf balls nestled in an egg crate, all painstakingly painted pink. He included a poem, hand-written on scroll after scroll of yellow legal paper, extolling my virtues but also poking fun at me. He was a man of contradictions. He loved his family, yet he was self-destructive when it came to his health. A half-pack-a-day smoker, he refused to quit. One evening, pregnant with my second child, I was sent into his basement hideout by my mother-in-law. She'd lured me there by saying, "It's our last chance, Helena. You have to make him stop."

I knocked on his door and entered when he said, "Come in."

"Sit down, Pook," he said, quickly getting up from his office chair and asking me if I wanted his seat.

I shook my head and perched on a stool with a green cushion, shifting my cumbersome last-trimester pregnant body into a position of least discomfort. "I need to talk to you, Poppy."

He leaned back in his chair, tilted his head to one side, and looked intently at me. "I know what this is about."

"Really?" I didn't think I was that obvious.

"They want me to stop smoking, and they sent you to do it. And you think because you're pregnant with my grandson, I'll listen to you."

"Oh," I said, deflated. "I had to try."

"Good for you, Pook. And you didn't insult my intelligence by pretending you didn't know what I was talking about." He smiled at me.

I smiled back. Poppy and I were always honest with each other. He liked to say that we were both straight shooters, as the cliché goes. I see now that we had an unusual relationship. I could have frank conversations with Poppy and know that I'd been heard. Not listened to, perhaps, but always heard.

Stubborn, I didn't want to give up, so I cried, which isn't hard to do when you're pregnant and emotionally labile. "Please, Poppy, why do you smoke cigarettes when it's killing you? Please, stop for your sake and your grandkids. Don't you want to see your grandson grow up?"

He handed me tissues calmly, shaking his head. "You know that this is emotional blackmail, right?"

I cried harder, thinking about a world in which he didn't exist anymore, feeling bereft for my children who wouldn't know their grandfather. I think I was projecting my own loss of not having my grandparents when growing up in Uganda and the United States, cut off from the benefits of being raised by an extended family. A village, so to speak.

Without Poppy, I'd lose a father too.

He came over and patted me on the back, giving me more tissues. "Come on, Pook, it's not that bad."

I kept sobbing. He sat listening but didn't try to stop me.

"I want you to be around for my kids, Poppy," I said, wiping my face, blowing my nose.

"I will be," he said with certainty.

I believed him, not imagining he would be dead before his sixty-first birthday, not knowing how heavily smoking had contributed to his heart disease, his heart so enlarged that it struggled to beat until it could no longer.

"I love you, Pook, and I love Erin and that little boy you're carrying. But I love to smoke and I'm not going to quit. It's one of the few joys in my life." He said this without a trace of regret in his voice or face.

Strangely, I respected his obstinacy and his forthright admission of his terrible habit. I have this sneaking suspicion that I really married SS because of how much I liked his father. Poppy and I were of the same sensibility. Doing for our families. Apologizing for not doing more. Not taking credit. He could be gregarious, but he was an introvert like me, preferring to be reading than attending a party. He allowed his wife to be in the limelight, allowed her to cast him as the villain. One of the first stories I heard repeated often and in front of their circle of friends and extended family was this from her: "When I go to meet Saint Peter at the pearly gates, he's going to say, 'BS's wife? Come on in! DS's mother? Bring a friend.'" His wife thought she was such a saint for living with Poppy that she would gain entrance to heaven. And she thought her daughter was such a burden to her that she could bring along a friend into heaven. But her son? She thought he was Jesus Christ—which, I suppose, means that I was Mary Magdalene.

Poppy didn't share her extreme opinion of his son, but Poppy was proud of him. It was not because SS was a doctor. Poppy told me he was proud of both of us because we had such great kids, made such a great family. He valued family above all else. He told me that he wished he had done a better job with his family, done a better job as a father. Poppy had attended every baseball game his son played in and almost every swim meet his son competed in, but he still felt he could have been a better father because he had worked at two other jobs besides his day job. He didn't indulge in guilt or self-recrimination like I did when I missed my children's first words or first steps, but he felt he had missed things he shouldn't have with his children.

He was always there for my children. For me.

In Central Park, the sound of bagpipes blared to my right, but I couldn't stomp through the tall hedge in the way. I walked quickly to where the hedgerow ended, swerved onto concrete from paved stones, and followed the curved path. The bagpipes seemed to recede, which didn't make sense. I wasn't getting closer; I started to run. I didn't care what I looked like—desperate, frantic. I felt like I had been going around in circles.

When I saw a low hedge to my right, I peeked over, looking for the bagpiper. There were a few heads above my eye level but no pipes sticking up into the air. Suddenly the music stopped. I whirled around, thinking I could still find the bagpiper, but there was no one even close to me. I was about to turn around and leave when a blur of colors caught my eye. I stepped through a black wrought iron archway with pink climbing roses dangling down. I entered a wide-open space with a fountain in the middle. I would learn later it was the Untermyer Fountain, and I was in the Conservatory Garden of Central Park. Three bronze figures cavorting, spraying water, riveted my gaze. I don't know why. *Happiness,* I thought. I slowly approached the figures, wary. *Are they going to disappear too?* The wind blew and water splattered onto my running shoes, drizzled my legs. I kept walking toward the grounded figures, a sculpture of three young women holding hands, dancing in a circle, unrestrained. The utter joy of it. "Love is eternal," I heard a voice say, loud and clear. It wasn't Poppy's voice, but I knew it was him. He had always given me reassurance when I was uncertain, told me that he was proud of me when I thought I was fucking up. And now he was trying to tell me that the three of us—Erin, Liam, and I—were going to be okay. That we were going to survive this. That this agony, too, would pass.

I still believe it. Even though the scientist in me remains skeptical and sometimes tries to convince me that my encounters with Poppy were visual and auditory hallucinations. But deep in my heart, I still believe that a dead man was trying to reassure me. To remind me that I am loved.

Chapter 17
Legacy of Abuse

My sister was fifty years old before she told me she had been sexually abused. It was our math tutor while we had been detained in Uganda, languishing at the Kampala International Hotel. She was thirteen years old. He was a man in his thirties with a wife and three children.

"Did he touch you?" My sister stared into my eyes, her pupils like pinpoints.

I looked away. "No, no, of course not."

I thought repeating the denial would protect me. I felt a burning in my stomach and a stab of pain at my temples. I squinted against the light, dreading the onset of a migraine. I took a gulp of my quince tea at the bakery café in Koreatown, hoping the warm liquid would fill the hollowness.

It must not have happened.

Did he touch you?

Her question echoed in my head. It popped up at the most inconvenient times: walking amid cherry blossoms at the reservoir in Central Park, navigating Grand Central Terminal at rush hour. Waiting to cross the street in Harlem four years after our conversation, a blinking red hand having turned me into a statue while swarms of people walked around me. A sudden chill burrowed into my body on a hot summer day, goose bumps on my forearms, the hair on my legs raised. I pressed my lips between my teeth to stop them from chattering.

An image I could not shake away: a bright-red blossom on the balcony of our hotel room in Kampala; my sisters with their heads bent over their schoolwork in the shade; me looking out the sliding glass doors into the garden. *I just want to be in sunshine.*

He coiled his arms around my thin nine-year-old body, trapping me. He tried to kiss me, missing my mouth as I jerked away. I hated the loud smacking of his puckered lips. I abhorred the bristle of his coarse mustache against my cheek. I held my breath but inhaled the stench of cigarettes wafting from his mouth. I tried to use my long, straight hair as a shield, but the spice-like odor of his aftershave, the stubble of his face chafing against the delicate skin of my neck, his guttural moans, assaulted me.

The scent of cardamom and cumin still make me want to vomit.

So when my son told me what happened to him, I wallowed in denial, hoping and wishing none of it was true. That desperately wanting none of it to be true was somehow more important than my son's safety.

I talked to my son's therapist at the time, a man who waved away my concerns. A man who told me these "dreams" were manifestations of my son's anxiety because he was "caught between his parents." What the man said did not sound right to me, but I believed him because he had a doctorate in psychology—he was the expert. In retrospect, I think: *What an idiot.* Yes, I'm talking about him, but I'm also talking about me.

I cried for days after Liam said he wanted to file a police report. Sometimes suddenly, without warning. While drinking coffee in the morning, while lifting a spoonful of rice to my lips at dinner. Sometimes I could feel the itching of my nose, the scratching at my throat, the inevitable fall of tears. Sometimes I howled. Sometimes I whimpered. I was leaking and pouring grief.

I refused to meet with Liam's counselor at first. It is to her credit that she persisted. And Liam persisted. When I finally agreed to a family therapy session, I wailed, "I can't change what happened to him. He's not going to get justice. Why bother going to the police?" She displayed remarkable patience. She simply said, "He needs to have his voice heard. What you can do now is support him."

On August 25, 2015, my son and I went to a police station. I felt like I was in a bad episode of a police procedural. Except the reality was worse. The hallways had no natural light, and the fluorescent bulbs cast shadows. The cement walls and floors looked sickly gray. The metal chairs lined up in a row, which served as the waiting area, only heightened the rising panic in my body the moment I entered that building. No matter how many times I swallowed, the bile refused to stay down. No matter how many times I gulped for air, I could not get enough breath into my lungs. I remember thinking, *I love my son. But I hate this.* I would have run away screaming from that place if not for my son's counselor sitting next to us. The warmth of her hand against the goose-bumped flesh of my arm soothed me when I felt like I could not bear one more moment.

I started crying as we climbed the stairs to the second floor of the precinct. I only intermittently stopped during the next five hours until we were finished, my face bloated beyond recognition. My son did not cry. His long, lean body stood tall. His voice remained firm. I marveled at his courage. I told his counselor that I wasn't that strong at his age; I wasn't that brave.

She said, "He is a remarkable kid."

I felt like I had been thrown into one of those Olympic-size pools that Liam raced in when he swam competitively. Flailing and choking on chlorine-stinging water, unable to keep my head up, my body sinking down. But Liam looked like he could cleave cleanly through water. Gracefully. Effortlessly. Like he could rise above, his arms arcing over his body in a gorgeous butterfly, his best stroke when he swam the individual medley. I was struggling in a pool of my own making; he was quietly moving forward into healing, processing his pain in a vast ocean of sorrow. I felt so proud of him, although I had no reason to be. I hadn't been supportive; I had to be persuaded. But his counselor was. She gave him the love and encouragement when he needed it. Now I wonder what my life would have been like if I'd had a person to confide in, a person who cared enough to help me.

When the last tear was wrung out of my body, I was a rag doll. I walked home with Liam, without any memory of which streets we used. I wasn't aware of what I was doing, but apparently I kept asking my son what he wanted for dinner. He answered me repeatedly. Finally he touched my arm and said, "Mom, are you listening?"

I stopped walking. I looked up as fading sunlight slashed across the windows of a beautiful brownstone in front of us. I turned to him.

"I'm sorry, I don't think I can hear anything right now."

"What's the matter, Mom?"

The image of me during my interview with the detective played like a movie over and over in my mind. No matter how many times I shook my head, or how many times I told myself I wasn't going to think about it, the looping image refused to go away. Sitting in the gray-beige room, the detective had said, "Don't blame yourself."

I wept. "I'm his mother. I failed to protect my son. Who should I blame?"

I should have known better. I was a pediatrician. I, of all people, knew that children could be abused by family members, friends, teachers.

I had been seeing a therapist at a domestic violence center and talked mostly about the terror SS was continuing to instill in me with his litigation maneuvers. How I was trying to combat his manipulations, his lies. I ugly-cried most of those sessions, tears and mucus mixing, not enough tissues to clean it all up. But after my son filed his report with the police, I began to talk about the math tutor. I thought it would be excruciating, that I wouldn't be able to articulate my abuse. Instead I felt relief. My shoulders didn't clench, my stomach didn't churn, my head didn't want to explode. I calmly told my therapist what had happened to me on a weekly basis for months when I was nine years old. It didn't occur to me until years later that what I was experiencing was a release. The letting go of a secret. I didn't have to blame myself anymore for what was done to me as a child. I could be free.

Chapter 18
A Korean Elegy

Mom, it's me."

She looked up. Her wide-brimmed hat tipped back, my face reflected on the surface of her large sunglasses. Her cheeks crinkled into a smile. *"Heeseon-ah! You came,"* she said in Korean.

My mother was the only person who called me by my Korean name: Heeseon. My three sisters still use Helena, as does everyone else who knows me, even my Korean cousins. When I visit Korea, I use my American name, even though it's a chance for me to reclaim my Korean name, my Korean-ness. Somewhere, something in me resists becoming Heeseon.

"Yes, I came to see you," I responded in English, her use of the affectionate form of my Korean name disorienting.

I smiled back at my mother, but my lips quivered. My mother lived in a nursing home in the middle of nowhere New Jersey. On my first visit, February 10, 2018, I was so nauseated by the smell of dying people and pungent institutional cleaner, lingering long after the floor was no longer wet, that I had to keep swallowing nonexistent saliva to stop myself from running to the bathroom and throwing up. It was my mother's eightieth birthday, and she had been at the nursing home for less than three months.

Every time my sisters visited, she begged to be released, to go back *home*. What was home? Did she even know where home was anymore? Police officers had found her wandering in downtown Edison, New Jersey, confused and disoriented, the previous August. The hospital psychiatric ward tracked down one of my sisters. My mother was diagnosed with dementia and depression and readmitted to the Carrier Clinic, the same acute-care psychiatric facility where she had stayed when she tried to commit suicide in 2004. After an involuntary six-week commitment, and then an additional voluntary six weeks, my mother was placed in this nursing home.

I found out what had happened to my mother when I got a phone call from a lawyer. A guardianship hearing had been scheduled, and the judge assigned him to be my mother's lawyer, to look out for her interests. My mother had been at a psychiatric institution for months, and my sisters had not informed me. I had to hear from a stranger how sick my mother was. The lawyer asked me if I objected to my sister Clara becoming my mother's legal guardian. I said I had no objections to Clara's new role.

However, Clara vehemently opposed my coming to visit Mom for her birthday. The other two said nothing. Nothing in opposition, nothing in support. Clara, who had not contacted me in years, called, texted, and emailed me several times in one day. Her singular message: your visit will destabilize our mother—you are not welcome. I came anyway. But not before asking the opinion of a friend whose mother had also been in a nursing home. "Helena, you're her daughter," she said. "Of course she wants to see you." But I'd listened to my sisters' narratives about me for so long that I had to confirm with an outside source that I was not harmful to my own mother.

On her birthday, my mother was standing in front of an old-model boxlike TV, changing channels manually, probably looking for one of her Korean dramas, when I stepped through her door. "Mom?" I said. *"Heeseon-nee?"* she said, repeating herself over and over, despite my nodding and saying yes. She could not believe that I was standing in front of her. Maybe she had imagined that moment so many times that it didn't seem real when it happened. I had the same feeling. We had not seen each other for over ten years. After my failed pilgrimage to her apartment in Edison, New Jersey, in 2005, any letters I sent to my mother went unanswered. After she moved to another apartment, she refused to leave a forwarding address. And I became too mired in a brutal divorce to have the emotional bandwidth to search for her, to plead with her to end her isolation, to engage with the world of the living, to no longer dwell on the past. If not for her trademark large-brimmed hat and huge sunglasses, I would not have recognized my own mother now. She wrapped her tiny skeletal hands around mine, squeezing them tightly, not letting go. Because my mother had never been a physically demonstrative person, I was surprised. Then she hugged me. At first I was stiff in her embrace, then my shoulders collapsed and my chest heaved. When I pulled back to look at my mother, her eyes were overflowing with tears.

During that visit, as she blew out candles and dutifully ate her birthday cake, I kept looking back and forth between her and my sisters, as though to reassure myself that this woman was indeed our mother. If they all sang happy birthday to her and believed this frail old woman with a sunken face was our mother, then she must be. If I looked carefully, if I stared intently, I could see traces of my mother as she had been. The same lift of her eyebrow when she was skeptical. The same tilt of her head. The same soft, delicate cheeks. The same stubborn chin.

"*I have money,*" she said when we were alone. "*I could live with you and Liam.*"

I could only shake my head.

After my divorce, I had lost the three-bedroom condo in Harlem, only blocks from Central Park. Now, miles and miles from the Jacqueline Kennedy Onassis Reservoir, I lived in a studio with my eighteen-year-old son, a pullout sofa serving as my bed, in less than three hundred fifty square feet. My sisters did not offer to subsidize an apartment large enough for my mother, my son, and me. And I was not looking to continue being a caretaker—I had been counting the years until my son went off to college so I could live in Paris like Hemingway did in his twenties, in the 1920s.

"I can't. I have no room," I said. I didn't want to live with her. Yet there was a part of me that wished it were possible. And I could not stop the tears running down my face.

My mother took my hands and held them, while tears slid down hers.

A few months after her birthday, my mother fell at the nursing home and had to be hospitalized for alarming mental-status changes. They thought she had suffered a concussion. She had actually fractured her arm and the orbital ridge of her cheek. In the CT scan of her head, there was evidence of a previous facial fracture involving her sinuses. A radiologist who looked at her films said, "It must have been excruciatingly painful." I had to close my eyes tightly against the image of my mother falling and smashing her face against a wall, collapsing on the floor. Her cries echoing in some white hallway of a sparsely furnished apartment, unheard by her daughters. The loneliness she must have felt vibrated in my chest, and I had to take deep breaths to stop myself from breaking down.

When I was six years old, living in Seoul, my mother had commanded our housekeeper to throw away a ragged doll I loved. I cried all the way down the hall from our apartment to the refuse room, clinging to the doll. When the housekeeper tore the doll away from me and threw it down the trash chute, I lunged toward the doll with my left hand. As she released the small metal door of the chute, my index finger got caught between the wall and the door. My finger smashed and bloody, I ran crying to my mother, hoping she would comfort me. I still remember the look of horror on her face, how loudly she shouted at me for being so stupid.

On a warm July morning five months after my mother's birthday, I left my apartment in Rockaway Park to get to the nursing home in time for lunch. I wanted to see my mother's eating habits, her patterns. My sisters had said that our mother was precariously underweight because she was not eating. When asked why, she refused to answer. I arrived at the nursing home and found my mother in the community room with other elderly Koreans, watching TV. We went back to her room, institutional blue wallpaper and a painting of gaudy flowers above her single bed. Her lunch tray held pureed rice and an unidentifiable brown mound claiming to be meat. I fed my mother teaspoons of rice. She seemed to enjoy my smiling at her and lifting the metal spoon to her mouth. She ate some Jell-O. She drank some Ensure. I thought I was making progress. I thought I could convince my mother to live again.

For dinner, almost the same exact tray was brought to her room. But this time, despite my coaxing, other than a spoonful of Jell-O, she ate nothing. Not even a sip of water.

I had not seen my mother since her eightieth birthday. I thought many times about her, about visiting her. I don't know why I didn't go. Maybe I couldn't bear to see her there, in that place without beauty. Maybe I was selfish. I was afraid she would ask to come live with me again. I didn't want to break my mother's heart. And I hadn't seen her in so many years that it had become more natural to think about her than to visit her. When Liam and my friends would ask, "Are you going to see your mother again?" I said yes. But I never said when. Even when she was in the hospital, I didn't visit her. I told myself she would only be there for a few days, and it was even longer by train and bus to the hospital than it was to the nursing home. None of my sisters offered me a ride, much less offered to pick me up at the train station.

In her room, we listened to opera—*La Bohème*, her favorite. Tears slipped from under her closed eyelids. Yet she remained soundless. I held my breath. I felt like glass was shattering inside my chest, the shards piercing and slicing my heart.

"Do you remember the time we went to the Met Opera and saw *La Bohème*? I was still in medical school."

She looked at me, nodded her head, and smiled. *"You did so well in school. So smart."*

I smiled back. "Yup, that's me. Brilliant," I joked.

She raised her eyebrows, her face serious. *"No, it's true, you were bright."*

My shoulders tensed at the prospect of her berating me yet again for leaving medicine, for choosing to be a writer. I thought she would say *"Do you think you're Hemingway?"* the way she did when I was nineteen years old and timidly proposed that I major in English instead of chemistry. I had been so blinded by my hurt that I never considered the root of my mother's statement before—was she jealous? Was being a writer something she had not been allowed to entertain as a possibility in 1950s Korea, when she was in college? As I contemplated these questions, a faint memory surfaced, an event I hadn't thought about in decades.

One late afternoon during my senior year in high school, I stepped into the kitchen of my home and didn't see my mother. The house was silent. I had left my father smoking leisurely outside the garage. My younger sister must have been taking the late bus home from middle school after track practice.

"Mom?" I called up the stairs.

No answer.

But the door to her bedroom was open, so I climbed up the steps and walked in, the carpet muffling my footfalls. I saw my mother seated at a window, hunched over a piece of paper, a pencil in her hand.

"What are you doing?" I asked.

She visibly jumped, putting her hand to her heart. *"Is it that late already?"* she said in Korean.

"This is the usual time Dad and I drive home."

She started folding the pieces of paper but didn't rush, as if she were reluctant to let go.

"What were you doing?" I asked.

She looked up, her eyes wary. Then she straightened her shoulders and said, *"I was writing. I'm writing a book."*

I was astonished by her answer. "You mean a novel?"

She nodded.

"A Korean novel?" I was still stunned.

I had never entertained the possibility that my mother was a writer. I had grown up seeing her reading books all the time—she read more than she watched television—but these books were in Korean, so I had no idea what they were about. She talked about Hemingway and Tolstoy and Isaac Bashevis Singer, but I wasn't really listening, too wrapped up in my narrow teenage world. And I had seen her writing on pieces of paper or paper napkins that she would quickly put away into a drawer or her purse. I had assumed they were laundry or grocery lists. When she revealed to me that she was a writer, I responded with callousness. I didn't ask her what her novel was about. I didn't ask her how long she had been writing. I asked her what she was cooking for dinner.

In my mother's room now, I said, "If I was smart, then it was because of you." I reached out and touched the backs of her hands, which were paper thin, her skin almost translucent.

"Mom, we need to talk. The nursing home says you're not eating. Why?"

She pushed back in her wheelchair, closed her eyes. No answer.

"We're all worried about you."

She kept her eyes closed.

"If you refuse to eat, then we have to consider nasogastric feedings. A plastic tube will be put into your nose and down to your stomach. It's going to be painful. Do you want that to happen?"

She opened her eyes and glared at me. She violently shook her head.

"Okay, okay. We won't do that to you."

She sighed, closed her eyes, and leaned back.

"But why won't you eat?" My question was an anguished cry, like an aria from *La Bohème*, soaring into crescendo and echoing in the stale air of the room.

Her eyes remained closed.

"Please, Mom. Why are you starving yourself?"

She opened her eyes and looked at me with unspeakable sorrow. I had to squeeze my eyes shut against all that grief.

I bowed my head. "I wish things were different." I tried to smile. "I wish you were not so stubborn."

She nodded back at me. She tried to smile, but her lips pressed into a straight line.

I got up and pulled a paper towel from the metal dispenser next to the sink. I pressed the grainy texture against my eyelids, as though that would stop my tears. I scrunched my face, as though that motion alone would stop my tears. I squeezed my nose shut between my thumb and forefinger, as though that would stop my tears. Futile.

We listened to Vladimir Horowitz play *Moonlight Sonata*. The repeating melody of Beethoven's haunting dirge always reminded me of a rainy day. And listening to it with my mother in this desolate space, I'd never felt so sad, so fragile.

"You played the piano so beautifully," she said.

"You would have too, if you had lessons like me," I said.

She shook her head. *"Heeseon-ah, you were truly talented."*

My mother was not prone to compliments, and this change in her behavior was unexpected. Regret flashed through my body, scorching and bitter. If only we could go back and be kind to each other. A loving mother and daughter.

What words of comfort would I have wanted when I was in pain as a child?

What words could I offer my mother now?

"It's okay to let go," I said, my voice steady and even.

She looked at me, tilted her head ever so slightly, an unfathomable expression in her eyes. She reached for my hands with both of hers and pulled them to her face, pressing my palms to her cheeks. She closed her eyes and repeatedly stroked her cheeks with my fingers. She must have missed the touch of a human hand. A daughter's hand.

"It's okay to let go," I repeated. "I don't want you to be in pain. I want you to know that I wish you had a different life. I wish you had made different choices. But I love you and I want you to be at peace." I tried to speak calmly, convey my thoughts with clarity. But my lips were trembling, my breaths uneven, my words slurring and stuttering.

She looked at me, her face open and vulnerable. The seconds were suspended in time. She nodded; she closed her eyes. Tears ran in straight lines down her cheeks and dripped off her chin. Her lack of words multiplied and expanded my despair. I caught my tears in my hands, but mucus slipped through my fingers, and I cupped my hands to contain the mess. I stood up and washed my hands, grabbed tissues, and offered her one. She shook her head. Her tears had already dried.

On the New Jersey Transit train back to Penn Station, I sat crumpled against the window and stared at suburban landscapes of single-family homes replaced by urban scenes of car repair shops, box stores, and McDonald's, rendered almost beautiful in the soft evening light. But I was haunted by my mother's face—caved in but calm, her eyes so tired and lonely.

A week later, on August 5, 2018, my mother died.

A month later, my sisters scattered her ashes from a boat in Incheon harbor, near Seoul. My mother had never expressed a wish to be buried at sea. She had expressed a wish to see her sister and brothers—she knew her parents were dead and did not talk about them—but she never said where she wanted to be laid to rest. When

I asked what she wanted done after her passing, she simply closed her eyes. I don't think she cared about her physical remains. Perhaps all she wanted was to be remembered by her daughters.

In the spring of 2019, I went to Jeju Island and stayed for a month. I thought of this island, "the Hawaii of Korea," as the one place my mother had been happy. She was here on her honeymoon with my father, the only time in their marriage without conflict. Before she gave birth to four girls, never a jangsohn. Before she left the country of her birth, never to return home again. Before she isolated herself and her loneliness became a disease and she tried to kill herself. Before she finally succeeded.

I tried to imagine my mother on *Jeju-do*, this beautiful archipelago of stunning seascapes and volcanic mountains. I imagined my mother eating at a restaurant specializing in abalone—raw, grilled, or in rice porridge—carefully placing the most succulent piece on top of her rice bowl.

I tried to remind myself how lucky I was to have had time with my mother before her death. To have told her that I thought she had tried her best, that I was thankful for everything she had given me. To have remembered those ephemeral moments of joy and startling beauty: When she scolded me but still sewed that pink-and-white dress so I could get an A in home ec in seventh grade. When she made chocolate cake with chocolate icing from scratch on my birthday, me helping to sift flour and cocoa and her stirring the dark cake batter into smoothness. How she loved listening to me practice the piano, especially when I played "Für Elise." How Beethoven was her favorite composer. How listening to Chopin's nocturnes would make her stop cooking and come out of the galley kitchen in our small apartment and lean against the wall next to the Steinway upright and close her eyes. How she made me watch *La traviata* and *Rigoletto* on PBS, even though I hated opera as a thirteen-year-old.

When I told her that I wished she had been more flexible and had tried to assimilate to America, she looked at me with infinite regret. As though she knew. As though she wished it had gone differently too.

I told her that I understood it must have been hard for her. For years she had hand made all our clothes and cooked all our meals, stretching my father's meager salary as a medical resident to cover our family of six. Yet she rarely complained. She stoically bore the hard times, hoping things would get better. She was familiar with suffering and tragedy. She had survived both World War II and the Korean War. I saw her as obstinate, but maybe she was scared. She was so afraid that she clung to superiority and disdain, rather than admit she didn't know what she was doing. She was bewildered by American culture, whose language and customs were almost antithetical to the Confucian one in which she had grown up. I wanted to say that I forgave her for all the mistakes she made—that every mother makes—but particularly for her isolation and how its effects rippled through my sisters and me. But I didn't think she needed my forgiveness.

I walked the Olle Trail of Jeju Island for miles, past the sea crashing onto porous volcanic rocks; past old stone walls and grazing horses; past the white lighthouses, stark against brilliant blue sky. I tried to process through my grief, to stop the sensation of my breath being crushed by the image of my mother's crumpled face when she asked to live with my son and me and I shook my head no. And when I witnessed a *haenyeo*, a stalwart female deep-sea diver, swimming out while clutching her orange-colored buoy, I wondered if my mother had seen the same sight when she was here. I wondered if she admired the haenyeo as much as I did. I would like to think so. Haenyeo have been around Jeju Island for centuries, scouring the seabed and harvesting shellfish and precious abalone in good weather and inclement, and in all seasons, including winter, always providing for their families. I remembered my mother standing at the concrete kitchen counter of our house in Kampala, her hands molding soybean curd to make tofu, pressing water through muslin cloth, smiling and urging me to eat another piece of gimbap, my after-school snack.

I went to Jeju Island to remember my mother. At her happiest. At her finest. Before everything fell apart. Because that is how I choose to remember my mother. To pay homage to the woman she had been, to the woman she could have been. To etch into my memory the one place she had experienced unadulterated joy.

Chapter 19
In Havana with Hemingway

Americans are arrogant," Julio says as he flicks his forefinger off the tip of his nose, tilting his head back.

We are driving in Julio's meticulously preserved 1951 black DeSoto with the GranCar logo on the passenger panel. We are on our way to Finca Vigía, the ten-acre estate that was Ernest Hemingway's home in Cuba from 1939 to 1960. I know Julio is joking with me because I just told him that I'm not American—I hold a passport but I wasn't born there, and English isn't my mother tongue. But I also said, "My son is a lazy American." Julio laughed.

I think he appreciates my sense of humor. Perhaps we have found common ground as a Korean and a Cuban. I like Julio; he seems like a younger brother to me. He likes to joke as much as I do. Life without humor isn't worth living. In Cuba, as a taxi driver and tour guide, he makes more money than his childhood friend, an internal medicine doctor whose salary is the equivalent of fifty US dollars per month. Such is the economy in a socialist country. If I had been born in Cuba, I wouldn't have become a doctor—my parents would never have pressured me into an occupation that made so little money. And then perhaps there would have been no need for me to abandon medicine at the age of forty to pursue writing. Being born in Korea to a surgeon has had many disadvantages.

I met Julio at José Martí International Airport, outside Havana, because our Airbnb host, Jacqueline, had arranged for him to pick up my son and me. The flight from New York was direct and only took three and a half hours, but I felt jet-lagged. Disoriented. I don't speak Spanish. Liam does—he's been taking Spanish language classes since kindergarten, and now he's eighteen. But to describe Liam's Spanish, I will appropriate what Jean-Christophe, a Frenchman I met at a writer's retreat in Montagne Noire, near the Pyrenees, once said about my French: "Helena, your accent is impeccable. Too bad you cannot say anything in French." Liam's Spanish sounds like a Spaniard's. Too bad he can't say many things in Spanish.

While I waited for Liam at the arrivals hall because he was coming from Washington, DC, I overheard numerous announcements in Spanish and panicked. Had I gotten in over my head? I had spent my teenage years in West New York, with a lot of Cuban expats, and seen a glimmer of the culture and adored the food—who doesn't love *ropa vieja*? Unfortunately, the only phrases in Spanish I learned from my classmates were curse words. But I was going to stay at a *casa particular*, a private home for rent, not a hotel; I was going to take Spanish lessons; I planned to wander around Old Havana looking for inspiration for my novel. I told myself that I was *not* an ugly American.

And I told myself that I did not come to Cuba to chase Hemingway. I had already done that in Key West for twenty years. Who would be so foolish? I'd come to Havana because of a Korean drama. I had been living with thirty-somethings in a Rockaway, New York, house share that had proven to be a disaster—at age fifty-four, I was more a den mother than a roommate. Cold and lonely with nowhere to go in February, I latched onto Cuba. I had been watching *Encounter* with Song Hye-Kyo, one of the prettiest actresses in Korea. In the K-drama, she plays a divorced woman who goes to Cuba for business and literally falls into the arms of a younger Korean backpacker. He reminds her of what she could have been if she had not been a dutiful daughter, forced to marry a chaebol heir, forced to be silent and obedient. Park Bo-Gum, known as Bogummy to millions of his Twitter followers, a most swoon-worthy Korean actor, plays the adventurous yet thoughtful and kind younger man.

In the first episode of *Encounter*, the light in Havana is dazzling. The colors of the colonial architecture are faded but beautiful, 1950s-era American cars lovingly maintained in bubblegum pink, avocado green, bumblebee yellow, tangerine orange, baby blue. Song Hye-Kyo is told that the best place to see the sunset on the Malecon is at Morro-Cabaña, so she tries to take a taxi there. But conveniently for the dramatic plot, the car breaks down and she ends up taking the ferry and walking up the switchbacks of a large hill to the Fortaleza de San Carlos de la Cabaña, the largest Spanish colonial fortress in the Americas. While she's resting against a stone wall, with a blister on her Achilles heel from the strap of her expensive high-heeled sandals, her designer purse is stolen. Undeterred, she continues without a penny and with a painful wound. There is no explanation as to how she paid the entrance fee of six Cuban dollars. Song Hye-Kyo is simply gorgeous in a deep-red dress.

After Bogummy rescues her from falling off one of the fort's ramparts, they spend an enchanted evening together. She drinks a beer and watches the sun set. Cuban dancers swirl and twist around her. The dying light casts everyone in chiaroscuro. He buys her dinner at Al Carbón, a *paladar* in Old Havana, and a Cuba libre in a salsa joint called Club Borges. (Liam and I went to the restaurant for dinner and it's actually kind of fancy, but I couldn't find any trace of the dance palace.) Song Hye-Kyo tries salsa dancing after repeated attempts at demurring, and she laughs as he twirls her around the dance floor. (I took a misguided salsa lesson with tall, blond Swedes and felt woefully inadequate.) She says later to her friend that she felt like Cinderella, caught under the spell of magic.

At the end of the night, they stand in Parque Central, facing the Gran Teatro de La Habana, a neo-baroque masterpiece of architecture, beautifully lit in the dark. He wants to ask her if she has a boyfriend; instead he puts her in a taxi bound for the Hotel Havana (in real life, the Hotel Nacional de Cuba). As she drives away in the dark, the lights illuminating Havana throw shadows onto her face. But she is smiling. Song Hye-Kyo's beauty brightens and fades with each gentle bounce of the beautiful old American car. Or at least that's how I remember it.

The television drama doesn't show the ruin, the flies, the grime of Havana. At one point, Park Bo-Gum sits on a parapet on the Malecon with waves crashing behind him, the sky an impossible blue. The camera doesn't pan to the smelly seaweed washed onto broken concrete. It doesn't linger on the beer cans, crumpled napkins, and crushed plastic bottles littering the square beside him. When I made Liam re-create the same pose on the same parapet so I could take a series of pictures, he balked after several minutes. Bogummy didn't complain, I reminded my son. Bogummy's ass wasn't wet, he retorted.

I cannot reconcile the beauty of Havana with the abject poverty. The dichotomy is too much for me. I have trouble accepting things—of this, I am painfully aware. Maricela, another host at my Airbnb, tells me that the government rations cooking oil. Electricity costs about one Cuban dollar per month per household because most Cubans don't have air conditioners or automatic washing machines—but still, they pay the rough equivalent of only one US dollar per month. Water is even cheaper, Maricela says, and so is cooking gas. The benefits of a socialist country. But as cheap as that sounds, the average salary in Cuba is only thirty-five dollars a month, and milk can be ten dollars and meat can be five dollars. Who in the United States can live on thirty-five dollars a month? As everyone in Cuba has said to me: *"Cuba es complicado."* Cuba is complicated.

Like my love of Hemingway. I have a complicated relationship with a dead white man. Hemingway is the second dead white man to whom I have an attachment—my dead father-in-law being the first. Perhaps they were both father figures to me because my own father was so lacking. I read Hemingway for the first time when I was seventeen, and he changed how I thought about literature. He is the single biggest influence on my writing. I still think *The Sun Also Rises* is one of the most terrible books in the world. I couldn't care less about Jakes Barnes and his white male privilege, or Lady Brett and her clan of spoiled expats living in Spain. But I think *The Old Man and the Sea* is one of the best books in the world. I love Hemingway's clean, spare prose in that novel. The heartbreaking story of an old man struggling with something beyond him, something he cannot control, which Hemingway whittles down to the basics of language and action. I remain ambivalent about the fact that I have such fondness for a racist, misogynist writer like Hemingway. The epitome of toxic masculinity.

When we arrive at Finca Vigía, Julio parks under the shade of a tree and tells us he'll wait there. He raises his hand to greet the other guides gathered under another tree. Julio says he's been to Hemingway's home so many times that he doesn't need to see it one more time. Liam and I get out of the car. As I walk up to the Finca, I imagine Hemingway roaring into the circular driveway after consuming several Papa Dobles, a daiquiri variation he invented at his favorite bar in Havana. I marvel that he didn't crash his car while driving under the influence. Or maybe he did, and the police kept it quiet because he was a famous writer and they wanted to protect him from himself.

I peer into the tiled entryway of the main house and don't feel the presence of Hemingway, which is weird because the house is preserved exactly as he abandoned it in 1960. Liam and I can't see much of the house, which is cordoned off and cannot be entered. We wander over to the remnants of a swimming pool, weeds growing in the cracks of concrete. Hemingway's boat, the *Pilar*, is dry-docked at the Finca. I stare at it and still feel no presence of Hemingway.

When we return to Julio's car, he asks how I liked Hemingway's home. I say that I was disappointed. I say that Hemingway feels out of my grasp. Julio says that we must go to Cojímar, the inspiration for the fishing village in *The Old Man and the Sea*. When he drives to the coastal town, he parks by a sandy beach. We walk to a bridge where the Cojímar River runs into the sea and where Hemingway originally kept the *Pilar*. Blue sky meets blue water in gradations of color that is stunning. A young man under the bridge tosses a fishing net into the water. I want to take a picture because this is exactly what I would expect in a sleepy fishing village. But he wears a stars-and-stripes bathing suit more appropriate for a lazy Fourth of July beach picnic in the US. How ironic.

Julio tells me that across the bridge there is a beautiful park where he used to come with his grandmother when he was a child. He says he learned to swim here. He says that his childhood was idyllic. The image of Julio as a small boy makes me smile. Julio didn't grow up in Cojímar, and he was born long after Hemingway left Cuba. But he lives in San Francisco de Paula, not far from Finca Vigía.

Suddenly I wonder if Hemingway could have seen Julio's house from his writing aerie at the Finca, a rectangular tower with large windows on all sides. A perfect writing room. I can finally conjure Hemingway: I see him walking over from his bedroom at the main house, climbing up the worn steps, turning to have a last look at the palm trees on his property before sitting at his enormous wood desk and clacking away on his typewriter. I can see light pouring into the room. The clear, impossibly bright light of Cuba.

After my trip to Cuba, I'm returning to Korea. To Seoul. I will see my aunt Emo, my mother's sister, again. I haven't seen her in more than a decade. When I left Seoul in 2006, I had been too awash in the grief of rediscovering my family, my homeland, that I reacted with silence. I did not contact my aunt. I let years go by while lying to myself that I would go back. "This year," I would say, year after year, and yet I never went back. I was too ashamed—I was now a divorced woman. I was financially struggling, no longer a doctor and not yet a published author. But 2019 finally became "this year." A return home.

I have spent almost a month in Cuba, and I feel more connected to it than most places I've lived in for more than a year. Maybe it's the history of Koreans in Cuba, displaced because of the Japanese occupation of Korea. Maybe it's Hemingway. Maybe it's because Cuba is complicated. In Havana, a meticulously restored baroque architecture building might stand next to a falling-down ruin. The smell of garbage and human discards can be overpowering, but then a breeze from the Malecon will sweep through, bringing the clean scent of the sea. Hearing the whistles of middle-aged men or the kissing noises of young men makes me roll my eyes, but seeing a father holding his young son's hand while the boy walks on the Malecon seawall makes me want to cry. Havana is heartbreakingly beautiful.

Chapter 20
A Return to Seoul

When I land in Incheon in April 2019, it is still dark. I wheel my carry-on suitcase through mostly empty corridors at 5:00 a.m. After clearing customs, I know I must find the express bus to the city center and get to the Airbnb I reserved. Trying to use my airline miles, I have taken a convoluted route from New York via Germany to get to Seoul. I left JFK on a Monday morning, and because I crossed the international date line, I've lost a day so it's already Wednesday. I am so tired that I feel like I'm operating in slow motion. I hear announcements in English and Korean and can't seem to understand either. I follow the pictures for buses and taxis. A blast of chilly air greets me when I exit the terminal, and I stand in the dark of Seoul. I speak Korean so slowly and carefully, like I'm six years old, that the woman at the bus counter takes pity on me and answers in English and points to where I should wait.

Dawn breaks over Seoul as I stare out the bus window. I wonder if I passed this many tall apartment buildings en route to Konkuk University in 2006, when I was in Seoul last. Were there so many billboards with famous Korean actors advertising everything from cell phones to washing machines? I can't remember. Everything seems unfamiliar. I catch a glimpse of Incheon harbor, the water gray and still, and wonder if any remnants exist of my mother's ashes, which my sisters scattered there last year. I had wanted to return to Seoul with my mother. When I left Seoul in 2006, I had promised my aunt Emo that I would, and now I cannot keep my word. But then, I hadn't even kept my word about keeping in touch with Emo.

I had been drowning in sorrow after seeing my aunt again after decades without her in my life, and having her treat me like a beloved niece—she called me every Sunday afternoon in my dorm room for weeks while I was studying at Konkuk University for the summer—that I responded to her love and kindness with inexplicable silence when I returned to America. I didn't send a Christmas card; I didn't call on New Year's Day; I didn't write one letter to her in thirteen years. I see now that I was incapable of processing my regret, my desperate wish that I had grown up in Korea. I should have seen a therapist when I got back to Pittsburgh and woke up weeping every morning for a month. But in 2006, I was still in denial about SS and my life, stubbornly holding on to the fantasy that I had a good husband, a good marriage, a good life.

In 2019, the day before I got on a plane to Seoul, I sent an email to my cousin Niki, Emo's daughter in Los Angeles, and asked for her mother's contact information. I thought I would call Emo after getting to Korea—that is, if Niki answered my email. I thought that since I would already be in Seoul, it would be harder for my aunt to refuse to see me. When my cousin called me instead of emailing, I was so nervous that I stuttered and stumbled that I was taking the concept of "last minute" to a whole new level and I didn't expect anything from my aunt. When my cousin said her mother was happy that I was coming to Korea, that she wanted to see me, the feeling of lightness that flooded my body was exquisite. *Oh, I haven't totally fucked up* was my thought.

On the bus to Seoul, my tired mind debates whether I should nap right away or go out and explore. I tell myself that I will decide when I actually get to the studio apartment that I've rented for the next three weeks. Sure enough, a tidal wave of exhaustion pounds into me as I stand in front of the queen-size bed. The sunlight flooding through a wall of windows is no match for my uncontrollably drooping eyelids. I crawl under the covers and pass out for twelve hours. When I awaken, it's dark again. I drink some water, use the bathroom, and go back to bed. The next day, Yunjeong, my aunt's older daughter, calls me on my cell phone. She invites me to dinner the following night with her and her mother and her brother, Joonseuk. She asks how I'm recovering from jet lag. I lie and say that I'm fine. I've been subsisting on kimbap from the convenience store downstairs and sleeping for hours and hours. Going to a restaurant and talking to people like a human being will be good for me, I say to myself. I do this to combat my anxiety. I haven't seen my aunt in thirteen years.

The Insa-dong section of Seoul still has many *hanoks*, traditional Korean houses (mostly converted to teahouses, restaurants, and bed-and-breakfasts), and wandering around the neighborhood feels like I've stepped back in time. I walk in circles around the vegan restaurant Yunjeong has suggested for dinner. I'm rarely on time, never mind early, but this time I'm fifteen minutes early. Yunjeong texts me that they're all running late and that I should go into the restaurant and wait. It is April, but the night air still has a chill. The Korean restaurant is traditional, so I remove my shoes upon entering. I am guided to a low table and sit on a cushion on the warm wood floor. I fidget with my cup of barley tea.

"Heeseon-ah!" I hear my aunt's melodious voice to my left. I turn my head.

Emo is walking quickly toward me, a smile on her face.

I smile back in response, getting up from my seat, bowing my head.

Emo clasps both my hands in hers and squeezes them.

I give her a hug before turning to greet my cousins, Yunjeong and Joonseuk, and give them hugs. I feel like crying but I smile instead.

Emo sits down at the low wood table, directly across from me. *"What kind of niece leaves Korea and doesn't send any word for thirteen years?"* she says in Korean.

I hear both my cousins say, *"Mom, no, please don't say that!"* But I'm not offended. I laugh. "I am so sorry. I am a terrible person," I say. Emo smiles back. *"Well, we got that out of the way. How have you been?"*

"My husband turned out to be a monster and I was stuck in divorce hell for ten years." I switch to English, knowing my aunt will not understand every word. "My mother was right that I should never have married him. She called him *ssiraegi-nom*. A trash person." I smile and change back to Korean. *"But it is all going to be okay. I have survived. And I get to see you here in Seoul."*

When she hears me say *ssiraegi-nom*, she closes her eyes and nods, as though she is saying, *"Yes, I understand."*

There is a quality about my aunt that makes me say what I really feel and think. I wish I had been honest with my mother more, and not just at the end of her life. But when I was younger, I was afraid of my mother. Afraid of her disapproval, afraid I couldn't meet her standards. She had expected so much from me, placed her ambition and dreams on me. But Emo is different. She's forthright but doesn't use her words carelessly. She isn't cruel. My aunt will tell me later that she was unlike her siblings growing up. She spoke up whenever she felt her mother was being unfair. She was punished with beatings and loss of privileges. But she didn't change. She refused to stay silent and obedient. I wish I had been more like Emo when I was young. I've paid too high a price for staying silent, for being a good Korean daughter.

"I can see you've been very busy since I saw you last. I'm glad you're doing well now," Emo says without irony or skepticism.

Her lack of judgment feels refreshing. Yet I'm still astonished that I don't have to justify what I've been doing with my life. Then I remember that Emo was the woman who told me that my mother's first suicide attempt was not my fault, who had advised me to live a good life. I felt like Emo had alleviated my burden of guilt about my mother when my mother chose to isolate herself and not answer my calls or letters or the front door when I knocked. Even though she had resisted my efforts, I still felt like I should have done more, tried harder. But Emo told me that how my mother chose to live her life was not within my control. Emo had said, *"Don't let the tragedy of your mother's life ruin yours. It's not your fault."* Those words had reverberated in my head for years. Maybe I've come back to Seoul for absolution. Again.

In the restaurant, I smile at my aunt. *"Yes, I am happy now."*

"Did you write that book you wanted?" she asks.

"Yes, I finally finished it."

"When is it going to be published?"

"Hopefully soon," I say, not getting into details about how I need to find a book agent first, then an editor at a publishing house who wants to buy my book, then for all the stars to align for my book to be physically out in world. I don't say to her that all of it feels insurmountable sometimes, but it is enough that I wrote a book.

"Still, it is a shame that you aren't a doctor. All that education. All that time and energy wasted," she says, shaking her head.

"It was not wasted, because I write about it. And is it not more important that I am happy writing? I was not happy as a doctor," I respond. Strangely, I feel no shame. I'm not defensive or angry. I'm just explaining why I left medicine. I smile at my aunt.

"It is very important that you're happy with your life. You only have one life. I'm glad you're living yours well." She nods and smiles.

I feel my aunt's validation, her acceptance of my choices, so acutely. She isn't pretending or placating me. She is genuinely happy for me. Of course, it doesn't stop her from asking me later in my trip why I can't practice pediatrics and also write books. I laugh and say that I'm not a good multitasker. I tell her that I can do well at only one thing at a time. She smiles back at me and does not mention it again.

"Why didn't you come last year with your sisters to scatter your mother's ashes?" Emo asks.

"I had no money to travel," I say, trying to keep my face neutral.

"Your sisters didn't help you?" Emo's body moves back almost imperceptibly, her eyebrows raised.

"My sisters didn't help me through ten years of my divorce. Why should they help me get to Korea?"

My words are harsh, my voice strained. But I don't elaborate on how deeply hurt I've been that I couldn't rely on my sisters for any kindness during my divorce. That I couldn't rely on them for any reassurance that it wasn't my fault, to lend me money when I was broke, to take my kids for a couple of hours when I was so sick of being a single mother that I wanted to scream, to help my kids feel loved when their father didn't. I've accepted the fact that I can't change my sisters or their behavior. I can only change my reaction to them and my distance from them. I'm grateful that my friends helped me through those long, lonely, brutal years. That I survived. I'm still processing through my pain and grief, something I suspect I will be doing for a while. Healing doesn't occur overnight, or even in years. Sometimes it takes decades. I wish it didn't; it does. But I'm moving forward with my life, finding beauty, seeking joy, growing and evolving.

Emo looks at me with compassion. I sense she understands what I've left unsaid. She changes the subject and asks about my flight, my health. She is curious about the research I'm doing for the novel I'm writing. My cousins join in the conversation. Joonseuk jokes that the fake bulgogi meat tastes nothing like meat. I say that Korean food is mostly vegetables anyway. Yunjeong insists that the spicy vegan chicken tastes exactly like chicken. It's better for you, she says. What's the point of making tofu taste like meat? my aunt says. If you're going to give up eating meat, then stop making vegetables taste like meat. We all laugh. We end the evening at a traditional teahouse, where my aunt asks me why I didn't order green tea when I love it so much. I say I'm so old now that the caffeine will keep me up. She drinks chrysanthemum tea because it is soothing—good for sleep, she says. She invites me to dinner the next Saturday at her apartment. But my cousin Yunjeong volunteers to cook pasta for everyone instead. She lives in the same apartment complex as my aunt.

The next Saturday, Yunjeong calls and tells me that her mother is making dinner for all of us because Yunjeong got caught up in grading papers and didn't go shopping for ingredients. She says that Emo is happy to be cooking Korean food for me. I bring German ice wine to my aunt's apartment because that's the only alcohol she drinks, but Joonseuk brings several bottles of white and red from France. All the cousins drink wine while Emo cooks furiously all the typical dishes for a party: clear glass noodles with vegetables, seafood and scallion pancakes, barbecued ribs, and so much more. She moves between the kitchen and the living room, bringing more food and clearing the empty plates, while her children and I sit at a lacquered low wooden table, eating, talking, drinking. She smiles at the three of us. I feel like I'm one of her children and desperately wish it were true.

Joonseuk takes a sip of his red wine and smiles at me. "I didn't know that a Museum of Japanese Colonial History in Korea existed in Seoul."

"How ignorant of you," I tease him. "You should go sometime. It's near the Ewha University campus. Do you know they've compiled a meticulous list of collaborators? There is a literal blacklist of Koreans who conspired with the Japanese during the occupation. I asked the director if anyone from Gwangju was on it, and there were no Kangs, thank god."

"Great! We're not traitors," he says.

"You know more about Korean history than we do," Yunjeong jokes.

I shake my head. "I was completely ignorant of history when I called Seodaemun Prison Museum to ask if they ran English-language tours. The man on the phone says, 'No, normally we don't, but there will be an English tour at nine o'clock tomorrow morning. You are welcome to join. Please arrive early.' But I get lost and get there exactly at nine and run into the lobby of the museum to be told that the rest of my party has not arrived. I'm so relieved I haven't missed the tour that I don't question what she means by 'the rest of your party.' Five minutes later, a group of at least fifty people pour into the lobby, trailed by TV cameras and people with microphones."

My cousins laugh.

"Did you go to Seodaemun on Thursday?" one of them asks.

"Yes!"

"Didn't you see the gigantic MBC studio stage?"

"No!"

"MBC has been broadcasting news and specials all year there. Thursday, April 11, was the one-hundred-year anniversary of the Republic of Korea as a country." My cousins look at me bemused that I know so little about the independence movement during the Japanese colonial period, like an American ignorant of the Fourth of July.

"First, the soundstage is not at the main gate of Seodaemun, so I had no clue. And the man on the phone didn't tell me that it was a special tour for the descendants of the Korean freedom fighters. I met Ahn Jung-geun's grandson." I continue telling them that the tour was given in English because the grandchildren and great-grandchildren of the revolutionaries imprisoned at Seodaemun are now scattered all over the diaspora: Germany, Australia, Argentina, the United Kingdom, the United States.

Both my cousins stare at me. "You met a descendant of Ahn Jung-geun?"

"Crazy, right?"

My cousins are astonished that I have met the grandson of an important political figure in Korean history—the equivalent of meeting a descendant of George Washington in America. Korea has existed for more than five thousand years, but mostly under the rule of kings and emperors. When Korea was forced under Japanese colonial rule in 1910, Koreans resisted by the tens of thousands. Japan built hundreds of prisons on the Korean peninsula to suppress independence.

Seodaemun was the largest and most notorious one in Seoul. On April 11, 1919, a group of resistance fighters formally declared a Korean government-in-exile in Shanghai, China. They wrote into existence a country called the Republic of Korea with a provisional constitution.

I didn't know any of this until I went to Seodaemun Prison Museum. I felt stupid. What Korean doesn't know the history of her own country? But my parents never talked about Korean history. They were too busy trying to survive life outside of their birth country. They were more interested in me and my sisters speaking English well, excelling in school, finding lucrative careers. They hung paintings and scrolls and placed vases in glass cabinets, treasured mementos of their homeland. But they didn't talk about Korea. Not its history, not its politics, not even why they left. Whenever I asked, which was not often, my mother would say it was because my sisters and I, as girls, would not have had the opportunities in Korea that we had in America. That we were lucky to be in America. I didn't know the real reason they left until Emo told me that my parents couldn't have a son. I remember feeling deep regret that I wasn't a boy and also sorrow for my parents. The shame of this one fact ruining their lives.

In Emo's apartment, I don't tell my cousins about the horrifying facts I learned at Seodaemun, the cruelly creative ways the Japanese captors tortured the Korean prisoners: pulling out their fingernails, breaking every bone in their feet so they couldn't walk, forcing them to stand upright for days in a claustrophobic wooden box, literally flaying the skin off their bodies. When I left Seodaemun, I had to sit on a bench in a park, staring at blue sky and tall trees, because I felt so fragile. Like a glass goblet that would shatter if anyone touched me.

The grief I felt about my utter lack of knowledge of things Korean reminds me of my first visit to Gyeongbokgung, the main palace of the Joseon dynasty emperors, in 2006. I remember stepping through the main gate and immediately being arrested by the sight of a wide-open courtyard of paved white stones. The dark tile roof of the palace sloped beautifully down to a wooden structure with huge columns painted green and red. I had a *Last Emperor* moment: *This is what it feels like,* I thought. I had seen the Bernardo Bertolucci movie when I was still in college. There is a scene with the last boy emperor of China running through the Forbidden City, pushing brightly colored curtains out of his way until the last curtain reveals thousands of his subjects prostrated in the gigantic courtyard. The little boy stops abruptly and stares. I can't remember the rest of the movie well, but this scene remains fixed in my mind. To see the vastness of a palace is mind-numbing. And I want to belong. I want to point to Gyeongbokgung and say, "That is where I come from." Sadly, I know more about the War of the Roses in medieval England and Henry VIII and his six wives than I do about Korean history, especially in the twentieth century. I have been colonized by the white gaze, white standards, white expectations.

Instead of talking about my sorrow with my cousins, I joke about my ignorance of Korean patriots. I don't say how inadequate I feel. And my cousins are so impressed with my introduction to the descendants of famous revolutionaries that they call to their mother in the kitchen. They tell her my story of being Forrest Gump, an accidental participant in a historic moment.

"She didn't know who Ahn Jung-geun was!" one cousin says to Emo. My cousins don't mean to be unkind. They are just flabbergasted by my lack of knowledge about things they have taken for granted their whole lives.

I smile and play the fool.

"Don't be silly. Of course you didn't know. You didn't grow up here," Emo says.

Relief courses through my body. Emo dampens my feelings of shame with a simple statement.

My aunt continues to provide me with solace, with validation, when she visits me on Jeju Island a few weeks later. As we climb the wooden stairs clinging to volcanic rock up to Seongsan Ilchulbong, the extinct caldera of the easternmost mountain on the island, I ask Emo for mercy and sit on a bench placed strategically on one of the many landings.

I pant, trying to regain my breath while Emo breathes evenly.

"Heeseon-ah, I've been thinking," she says.

I'm still breathing heavily, but I think, *Uh-oh.* I try to brace for impact. It seems to me that nothing pleasant comes from anyone thinking. Epiphanies are usually painful.

"It's not your fault that your sisters don't like you. Your mother shouldn't have shown her favoritism so blatantly. It only creates problems among siblings. They felt hurt by your mother's actions and they're taking it out on you. But they're grown women now, and they shouldn't behave that way. They must live their lives and you must live yours."

I release my long-held breath. I close my eyes. She's right; I must live my life. No one else is going to live it for me. Might as well make the most of it. I smile at my aunt.

"Thank you."

Emo nods. *"You know, your grandmother loved only your mother. She cried for days after your mother married and left Gwangju. The rest of us felt like we didn't matter. But I didn't let that stop me. I lived my life. What else are you going to do?"*

I am so delighted by what a pragmatic and incredibly unbitter woman my aunt is. I wish I could emulate her. No, I wish I could be her. Instead I laugh.

"Let's go to the top, shall we?" I say, standing up.

"You're still a young woman. You should be in better shape," Emo scolds.

I smile. "Yes, ma'am," I say in English.

After our long weekend together on Jeju Island, I sit with my aunt at the airport, waiting for her flight back to Seoul to be called. My cousin Yunjeong and her daughter have gone searching for a mandarin orange smoothie. The island is famous for its varieties of oranges, especially the kind that westerners call clementines.

I hold my aunt's hand tightly, the two of us sitting in adjacent fixed metal seats. I don't want to say goodbye. I'm going back to Seoul later today, then to New York tomorrow morning. Emo has invited me to stay the night at her apartment, but I've already booked a hotel. I really cannot face farewells with any grace. I hate them. I break down again and again. Besides, I tell myself, I cannot afford a puffy face for the twenty-hour journey on two different planes, crossing multiple timelines.

"Heeseon-ah, you need to suffer to become strong," my aunt says. *"A little bit. Too much is no good. I've become a strong person because I suffered. You're strong because you suffered. You're going to be fine."*

"You are right," I say. "I'm okay with how things are." I say this in English, to no one in particular. I feel no anger.

"I will miss you," I say in English to my aunt, tears welling up. I'm still uncomfortable saying sentimental things in Korean. It feels more natural to say it in English.

My aunt shakes her head at me. *"To cry is to be weak."*

I laugh. *"My mother used to say that a lot! I think my mother should have cried more. It would have been good for her. Then she would not have kept all those feelings inside. Secrets are bad for you."*

"I used to cry all the time," Emo says. *"My late husband hated that. Now I don't cry. It seems even the tears have dried up now that I'm old."*

"You are not old," I say right away. *"Please. You ran up those steps to Seongsan Ilchulbong while I was huffing and puffing with each step."*

Emo laughs, reaches her hand out and pats mine. She stands up and I follow suit. It is time. I paint a smile on my face and wave as she looks back at me before disappearing down the tunnel to her plane. I wait in front of a large picture window staring at the words Jin Air. I watch as the blue-and-brown butterfly wings of the airline's logo seem to flutter as the plane swings away from the gate. The jet fumes create a wavy exhaust that looks like water rippling in sunlight. I try not to cry as my beautiful aunt departs.

After I check into my hotel near Seoul Station (a quick express-train ride to Incheon Airport in the morning), I decide to go to Namsan—literally translated "south mountain"—which is in south-central Seoul. I went to Namsan with my aunt in 2006. She had scampered up the incline to Seoul Tower while I struggled to keep up. I smile remembering her admonishment to me to hurry up. I cheat and take the bus this time, but I still have the vertical challenge of walking from the parking lot to the base of the white cylindrical monument with glass observation decks and a spiky radio transmission tower at the top. I am out of breath when I reach the level where Korean lovers have attached metal locks along the railings and fence, mimicking what tourists have done on bridges in Paris. As the sun disappears behind the horizon, the blue hour drenching Seoul is stunning. Lights flicker on everywhere. I feel sad and happy at the same time.

I miss my son, so I call him on the phone. It's eight in the morning in Washington, DC, but I know he's still sleeping. He answers my call, mumbling, "Hey, Mom."

"Sorry to wake you, babe, but it's my last night in Seoul and I need to talk," I say, feeling selfish but not caring.

"It's okay. What do you want to talk about?"

I tell him that Seoul Tower has become a serious tourist attraction, with colored lights and merchants and music and a huge food hall. I tell him that I bought a gorgeous pair of earrings for a total bargain, the equivalent of ten US dollars, from a young Korean woman who taught herself jewelry design—I suggested that she export her jewelry to the US. I tell him I'm having a hamburger and fries like a tacky American, but it's all tasty because, of course, Koreans know how to really cook. We're a nation of foodies, I say. Liam laughs in the right places. He tells me that it's okay when I start to tear up about my aunt.

"Do you think you'll be back?"

"Yes," I say. Then I laugh. "But I say that every time I'm back in Seoul—well, all two times. But still. 'Next year,' I say, every year." I pause for a few moments. Liam doesn't push, waiting patiently on the line. "But I think this time it's different because I'm a different person. I feel a connection with Seoul that I didn't thirteen years ago. Not just with its history and its past that I didn't know about, but with the present. And I feel such a strong pull to know more, to push through my grief and discover a new me. A Korean me. Maybe it's my aunt, maybe it's the fact that I'm writing a novel about Korea. I feel like I could belong here."

As I explain to my son why I feel different, I don't mention his father and how SS constrained me for so many years, made me suppress who I was so I would conform to his idea of what a good wife should be. And I didn't know how much I wanted my son to connect with his Korean heritage, his ancestors. The only way for him to feel connected to this land was for me to feel connected to it. But I didn't feel rooted to it after I left Seoul as a child. My mother assumed I would identify as Korean because she said so, but she rarely talked about Korea or our relatives there or what our lives were like before we left. Our relationship was more Confucian, more like that of a monarch and her subject: my mother commanded; I obeyed. My relationship to my son is more egalitarian, more American. I don't demand; I suggest.

And I don't want to push away my Korean-ness anymore. I see how I am stronger with it.

Liam was in Korea when he was six years old. He hasn't returned since. Partly financial concerns, mostly a mother brutalized by a divorce with no emotional energy to guide him through the grief of not knowing his culture. I feel like it is now possible for me to help my son discover his Korean-ness, make whole a missing identity. I can become Heeseon again.

"I want you to come with me next year," I say.

"I'd really like that, Mom."

I feel like I can finally breathe. Big breaths in and out. Nothing stuck in my throat, no pressure on my chest. I laugh and tell my son that I love him and that I will see him in a few days in New York.

ACKNOWLEDGMENTS

I want to thank my agent, Amy Elizabeth Bishop, without whom this book would not be possible. Thank you, Amy, for believing in my book even when, sometimes, I didn't or couldn't. I want to thank my editor at Little A, Selena James, for taking a chance on an unknown Korean American woman writer.

Much gratitude goes to the early readers of my memoir who are also my wonderful friends: Angie Griffin, Julie Marie Wade, Rose L. Cirigliano, Lorena Savignac, Jeannie Fitch, Jolene McIlwain, Steph Liberatore, Susan Isaak Lolis, Maureen D. Hall, and Deb Gieringer. A shout-out to Jenny Forrester of Unchaste Press for nominating my essay "A False American Dream" for a Pushcart Prize. If not for you, Jenny, I might have given up on writing.

I owe a debt of gratitude to the writers Lidia Yuknavitch, Julia Glass, Mark Sundeen, Lee Gutkind, and Ira Sukrungruang for their memoir workshops and their insightful comments on my work.

Finally, I want to thank my son, Liam, for his love, generosity, and kindness. Thank you for loving me and my book, Liam.

ABOUT THE AUTHOR

Photo © Liam Studer

Helena Rho is a three-time Pushcart Prize–nominated writer whose work has appeared in numerous publications, including *Slate*, *Sycamore Review*, *Solstice*, *Entropy*, *805 Lit + Art*, and the anthologies *Rage and Reconciliation* and *Silence Kills*. A former assistant professor of pediatrics, Helena received her doctor of medicine in 1992 and has practiced and taught at top-ten children's hospitals: Children's Hospital of Philadelphia, the Johns Hopkins Hospital, and Children's Hospital of Pittsburgh. She earned her MFA in creative nonfiction from the University of Pittsburgh. For more information, visit www.helenarho.com.